I will, with God's help

Episcopal Confirmation for Youth and Adults

Leader's Guide

by Mary Lee Wile

Living the Good News
a division of the Morehouse Group
600 Grant Street, Suite 400
Denver, CO 80203

Living the Good News
    a division of The Morehouse Group
Editorial Offices:
600 Grant Street, Suite 400
Denver, CO 80203

Cover Design: Jim Lemons
Cover Photograph: Regan MacStravic
Page Design: Vicky Rees

Printed in the United States of America.

The scripture quotations used herein are from *The New Oxford Annotated Bible with the Apocrypha, Revised Standard Version.* © 1973, 1977 by Oxford University Press. Used by permission.

Excerpts from *The Book of Common Prayer and Administration of the Sacraments and Other Rites and Ceremonies of the Church,* published by Church Publishing Corporation, 1979.

ISBN 1-889108-73-1

Table of Contents

ACKNOWLEDGEMENTS

One of the delights in working on this project has been the time spent in conversation with Episcopalians around the country, as well as the time spent listening to the witness of Christian writers and thinkers throughout the ages. It has made me deeply aware of our interconnectedness; it has given new meaning to "the communion of saints." My gratitude extends far beyond those named below or listed in the bibliography to students, teachers, mentors, colleagues and friends who have informed my thinking and shaped my believing.

Sine quibus nullus liber: the Rev. Robert Jewett, the Rev. Vicki Sirota, the Rev. Lewis Sligh and the Rev. Leslie Smith. Without their gracious and insightful collaboration, there would indeed be no book, no program.

Others whose input has proven invaluable include the Rt. Rev. George Cadigan, the Rt. Rev. Chilton Knudsen, Brother Curtis Almquist, S.S.J.E., Caroline Black of Grace Calvary Episcopal Church in Pittsburgh, Betsy Boyd of the National Youth Ministry Office; Dina Strong Gluckstern and Liz Riggleman of Living the Good News, the Rev. A. Katherine Grieb, Youth Missioner Jane Hartwell, the Rev. John Lathrop, Brother Eldridge Pendleton, S.S.J.E., the Rev. Wendy Rozene, the Rev. Ellen Shaver, Professor Robert Sherman, the Rev. Daniel Warren, and Elizabeth Ring, Director of Maine's Diocesan Resource Center, whose time, energy, knowledge and good humor sustained me on this journey. Special thanks to my Godson, Zach Gluckstern, for his help with the Youth Journal.

And without the support, encouragement, companionship, care (and cooking) of my husband Rick Wile, I couldn't have completed this project in the midst of full time teaching. He provides bread for the journey, in more ways than I can name.

Christianity, I keep hearing and reading, is communal; we are all part of Jesus Christ's extended family, brothers and sisters through faith. What a gloriously diverse and deeply caring family it is! I extend heartfelt thanks to all who have been part of this project.

Foreword

A BISHOP REFLECTS

He is what we used to call a "cut-up," a clown who seems to take nothing seriously. Down in the undercroft before the liturgy, he was restless and distracted, disrupting the reverent "Bishop meets with confirmands" time the priest had so carefully orchestrated. Here we are now, wrapped within the mystery of liturgy, the renewal of baptismal vows still echoing in the air. Carrying himself with a mixture of awkward self consciousness and youthful dignity, he kneels before me on the chancel step, parents and sponsors touching his shoulders. I lay my hands on his head, pausing for a moment before praying:

> *Defend, O Lord, your servant Peter with your heavenly grace, that he may continue yours forever, and daily increase in your Holy Spirit more and more, until he comes to your everlasting kingdom. Amen.*

As he rises from the step, his face glows. His shoulders straighten. He looks me in the eye with a grin and whispers, "Cool." At the exchange of the Peace, we hi-five one another.

I am at a hospital bedside. She had planned to be received into the Episcopal Church that morning, because "After 78 years, I decided that I want to belong." She was rushed to the hospital two days ago. Having told her priest to "bring the Bishop over here no matter what," she now uses every bit of available energy to affirm the ancient vows. I take her hands gently, careful of the IV tube, marvelling at the firm grip under the tremble:

> *Eleanor, we recognize you as a member of the one holy catholic and apostolic Church, and we receive you into the fellowship of this communion. She closes her eyes as the prayer continues, my hand on her forehead, God, the Father, Son and Holy Spirit, bless, preserve and keep you.*

A great peace settles upon us, priest and bishop and newest member of the Body of Christ. Her eyes remain closed, tears flowing soundlessly. The priest touches her eyes gently with the edge of a tissue. Together we use up many tissues in the moments which follow.

One letter stands out in the always-thick file of incoming mail. It tells of a mother and daughter, once estranged in a painful tragedy of family division. The daughter plans to reaffirm her baptismal vows, a decision which represents a long journey indeed. Her mother writes that she wants to join her daughter and do the same. In the tiny church where these reaffirmations are to take place, the details of this reconciliation are well known. The day arrives. The daughter, a single mother, kneels with her toddler son alongside, as I pray:

...May the Holy Spirit, who has begun a good work in you, direct and uphold you in the service of Christ and his kingdom.

The toddler rocks back and forth on his heels, holding onto his grandmother who kneels while the prayer is offered over her next. At the exchange of the Peace, the mother takes off the antique heirloom cross she was wearing to slip it over her daughter's head.

In the midst of current explorations regarding the theological and pastoral significance of confirmation, reception and reaffirmation, moments like these provide the best foundation for our evolving consideration. These rites enfold our human journeys, all past and future moments, into the Body of Christ, the Church. These rites gather it all—our reconciliations, our tears and our hi-fives—into the awesome mystery of belonging to Jesus Christ. These rites solemnize decisions made, life-directions chosen, loyalties embraced.

It is the sacred privilege of the Bishop, standing in continuity with the apostles, to act on behalf of the entire Body of Christ through the liturgical events which recognize and affirm these commitments, made in the context of the entire community's renewal of the Baptismal Covenant. Each day I pray for all those I have confirmed, or received, or for whom I have witnessed the formal reaffirmation of baptismal vows, entrusting them corporately to the Savior whose grace has stirred them to this bold declaration of self-surrender. I pray that the faith community, the Body of Christ in every place, will challenge and comfort them through the continuing journey of their lives. I pray that they will ever be shaped by the transforming moment when I laid hands on them and the claim of Christ upon their lives was vividly apparent.

A COMMENDATION

This program of formation for confirmation, reception and reaffirmation of baptismal vows, appropriately titled *I will, with God's help*, offers a remarkable synthesis of those elements of formation which undergird these rites. In this program, Mary Lee Wile brings together the vital themes of belonging, community, prayer, repentance, Scripture, service, story and worship. Her suggested activities foster simple, profound experiences of the holy. Leaders of such programs of formation will welcome her concrete advice and tender affirmation of their ministry. Her guidance recognizes the importance of experience as a primary learning avenue for the Christian journey, while affirming the gifts of our received tradition: our sacramental theology, our worship, our love for the Word. Every "yes" we make to Christ is grounded in God's "yes" to us, whose name is Jesus Christ, in whose Body we live out our days.

— The Rt. Rev. Chilton Knudsen, Bishop of Maine, February 5, 2000

Introduction

CONFIRMATION

"You have to have room for me!" the rumpled businessman insisted. "See? Here's my confirmation number. I have a confirmation number!"

Nearly midnight on a Tuesday in early December, and there was no room at the inn for that weary traveler, nor for my husband and me waiting in line behind him. A security guard finally drove us to a seedy motel across town.

In "What Shall We Do About Confirmation?" Leonel Mitchell ponders giving up the word "confirmation" altogether. For some Episcopalians, the meaning of confirmation seems as vague as those hotel confirmation numbers, as uncertain as that young security guard driving through midnight. Despite carrying our uncertainties like so much battered luggage, however, ultimately most Episcopalians continue to claim confirmation as both valid and valuable. The opening rubrics of the confirmation service point out that those baptized young are "expected" to be confirmed, and even Mitchell ends up seeing it as "the rite in which those baptized as infants have the opportunity to own the faith in which they have been brought up" (107).

Besides those who have grown up as "cradle Episcopalians," a number of today's confirmands are adults from other traditions, confirming their membership in the Episcopal Church by reaffirming their baptismal vows.

A Personal Note to Leaders

Be tender to yourself. Taking on leadership of this program involves time and energy; find ways to replenish yourself. Trust the Spirit to be with you in this endeavor, but also honor your own, other needs during this time. Sessions are set up to offer choices, to involve participants as much as possible, to allow you to be facilitator rather than choreographer. Youth Missioner Jane Hartwell says that leaders of any program need to be fed by the process or they won't keep doing it. Find ways to be fed.

Consider seeing yourself as participant as well as leader: you may want to reaffirm your own Baptismal Covenant when the participants confirm or reaffirm theirs. Join Roberta Bondi in her anxious prayer:

> My God, anxieties over what might happen a year from now overwhelm me. Help me remember that I actually face the future best, most flexibly, with the most integrity, most in accordance with the actual needs of others and myself, if I can let go of my desire to control what I cannot control so that I can respond appropriately to what might actually happen (84).

In their catechetical *Questions on the Way*, Tucker and Swatos remind all baptized Christians that they are already "saints": those who "through Christ...have received the gift of the Holy

Spirit and are striving to press on to the likeness of Christ, no matter how far from the goal they may be" (46). With that understanding, you are a both a saint and the leader of saints. As leader, you are also God's witness, but certainly not the only witness your participants will have. God, after all, is free to speak to them through many other voices and ideas. Karl Barth once said that God can speak his Word to us "through Russian Communism, a flute concerto or a dead dog." Barbara Brown Taylor echoes Barth more gently by suggesting that holiness may be found in "a green leaf, a clay cup, a clean sheet, a freshly sawn board; it may be just below the surface of a key, a clock, a shiny stone" (33). In other words, God is really the One in charge (even though you are the one who will set up each session).

A BACKWARD GLANCE AT BAPTISM

Those seeking confirmation, reception or reaffirmation of baptismal vows have already been baptized. Baptism, says seminary professor Robert Sherman, is an absolute, grounded reality in which we are marked and sealed. It is God's initiative that brings us to Baptism, whether it is through moving our parents' hearts or our own. Confirmation acknowledges and accepts that reality.

The Standing Liturgical Commission states: "There is one, and only one, unrepeatable act of Christian initiation, which makes a person a member of the body of Christ" (120); that rite is baptism. Over the years, some have tended to see confirmation as a sealing with the Holy Spirit, a final piece of the initiation process begun at baptism, but that is wrong. Confirmation is the renewal of one's Baptismal Covenant, not its completion; "confirming and renewing [baptized persons] in their baptismal promises is not the same as adding another injection of the Holy Spirit" (Micks 37). Baptism is complete in its own right/rite. As the prayer book says, "The bond which God established in Baptism is indissoluble."

Ellen Charry reminds us that at baptism we "are grafted into the divine life, sanctified by being chrismated—signed with oil—by the Holy Spirit and marked as Christ's own forever" (By 372). Taylor echoes this: "...my vocation is to be God's person in the world...The instant we rise dripping from the waters of baptism and the sign of the cross is made upon our foreheads, we are marked as Christ's own forever" (29-30).

From the moment of baptism, we belong fully to Jesus Christ. The waters of baptism both wash and welcome us. Jesus tells us, "You are not of this world," and it is this sacrament that separates us out and gives us to God. The "Thanksgiving over the Water" prays:

> We thank you, Almighty God, for the gift of water. Over it the Holy Spirit moved in the beginning of creation. Through it you led the children of Israel out of their bondage in Egypt into the land of promise. In it your Son Jesus received the baptism of John

and was anointed by the Holy Spirit as the Messiah, the Christ, to lead us, through his death and resurrection, from the bondage of sin into everlasting life. We thank you, Father, for the water of Baptism. In it we are buried with Christ in his death. By it we share in his resurrection. Through it we are reborn by the Holy Spirit....

In St. Augustine's time, those preparing for baptism went without baths for 40 days, partly because public baths were places of temptation, but also partly to increase awareness of what they were preparing to do. They were, however, required to bathe on Maundy Thursday to rid themselves of "unpleasant smell" and to ready themselves for the sacrament. In her book on baptism, Marianne Micks closes her introduction by stating that "entering into baptism is entering into deep waters with excitement and joy" (xiv). Confirmation, then, represents a mature recognition that we are awash in these deep waters, surrounded by grace, cleansed and buoyed up by the Holy Spirit.

Baptism, however, is more than a refreshing swim in the river of God's grace. As liturgist Daniel Stevick says, "Baptism is—or ought to be—a commissioning for ministry; it is strength for spiritual combat; it is the ordination of the laity" (qtd. in Micks 93). As early as the 1552 prayer book, the confirmation prayer is for ongoing "strengthening" by the Holy Spirit, which our current prayer book continues:

> *Strengthen them, we pray, with the Holy Spirit that they may grow in grace. Increase in them the spirit of wisdom and understanding, the spirit of discernment and inner strength, the spirit of knowledge and true godliness, and fill them with wonder and awe at your presence, through Jesus Christ our Lord. Amen.*

Nothing "new" happens at confirmation, but through the bishop's participation in the rite, confirmands are physically connected to the diocese, the Episcopal Church and the Anglican Communion, and "are sacramentally united with the apostles, the universal Church, and with Jesus Christ" (Tucker and Swatos 79).

Last winter at a Chinese restaurant my fortune cookie held the message: "You will get some new clothes." It seemed the silliest fortune I'd ever gotten—until I reread Ephesians and was reminded that we Christians are to be clothed in the armor of God. Then I encountered the Tuesday morning Epistle Reflection in the New Zealand prayer book which states:

> *baptised into union with Christ,*
> *we have put on Christ like a garment* (115).

Confirmation is a time to acknowledge this gospel wardrobe, to make a public "fashion" statement.

A BRIEF LOOK AT CONFIRMATION

The rite of confirmation itself, says Charles Lowry, has "both ancient, continuous tradition and pragmatic psychological effectiveness" (120). In other words, confirmation both honors tradition and is genuinely good for us. Ellen Charry agrees that "knowing and loving God is the mechanism of choice for forming excellent character and promoting genuine happiness" (By 18). Preparing for confirmation and thereby claiming as our own the words of the Baptismal Covenant can be life-enhancing.

Lowry traces confirmation back to the early church as recorded in Acts. Marianne Micks, however, goes back even earlier, seeing in the renewal ceremony Joshua held at Shechem a prototype for confirmation. Joshua charged those who had entered the Promised Land to renew their commitment to God by affirming the covenant enacted at Sinai: "Choose this day whom you will serve," Joshua told them. This is what Christians do at confirmation, says Micks, when they are "given an opportunity to choose yet again the One whom they will serve" (76).

Confirmation is a public, voluntary reaffirmation of Christian identity. The presentation of candidates for confirmation in the Australian prayer book is followed by a section labeled "The Decision." Here the candidates are told, "Before God and this congregation, you must affirm that you turn to Christ..." (87).

The Rt. Rev. George Cadigan encourages bishops to ask each candidate, "Why are you doing this? Do you mean to be faithful and loyal in attendance?" Confirmands should become familiar with the commitment they agreed to or that was made for them in the Baptismal Covenant and which they will affirm in confirmation. Bishop Cadigan hopes that confirmands come to the rite for the sake of faith, love and conviction.

Preparation for confirmation, reception or reaffirmation of baptismal vows should be done freely, without peer pressure. The Rev. Wendy Rozene speaks of confirmation as a personal commitment, an acknowledgment of the relationship between the confirmand and God. Cadigan, Mitchell and Rozene all stress that a leader must be willing to let participants say "no" or "not yet" to confirmation, even after a long period of preparation. Leaders of both adult and youth programs need to trust the Holy Spirit's work among the participants, Mitchell says, "recognizing that some baptized communicants may never be ready" (107).

In its 1973 Prayer Book Studies 26, the Standing Liturgical Commission offered the following insights about Confirmation:
1. An act and occasion for (more or less) mature personal acceptance of promises and affirmations made on one's behalf in infancy is pastorally and spiritually desirable.
2. Such an act and occasion must be voluntary; but it should be strongly encouraged as a normal component of Christian nurture, and not merely made available.

3. It is both appropriate and pastorally desirable that the affirmations be received by a Bishop as representing the Diocese and the world-wide Church...

4. The rite embodying the affirmations should in no sense be understood as being a 'completion of Holy Baptism,' nor as being a condition precedent to admission to the Holy Communion, nor as conveying a special status of church membership.

5. The occasion of the affirming of baptismal vows and obligations...is a significant and unrepeatable event. It is one's 'Confirmation Day.'

6. The rite, however, is suitable, and should be available on other occasions in the lives of Christian people (4ff).

The document goes on to speak of those who have fallen away from the church and wish to make a public affirmation of their return. Hence, those who may have been confirmed at some earlier point may wish to reaffirm their commitment and/or be received into this particular denomination through a public ceremony. The 1979 *Book of Common Prayer* uses the same service for all three options: Confirmation, Reception and Reaffirmation. This program is suitable for all three.

RECENT REALITIES CONCERNING CONFIRMATION IN THE EPISCOPAL CHURCH

Jane Hartwell tells a joke about the bat-infested belfry of a Baptist church: The resident pastor called exterminators, but the bats refused to go. Several other Protestant ministers came and prayed for them to leave, but the bats refused to go. The Roman Catholic priest tried exorcism, but the bats refused to go. Finally the local Episcopal priest said, "I know what will get rid of them." The bishop came and confirmed the bats—and they were never seen again.

What the joke names is the documented loss of Episcopal young people who view confirmation as graduation *from* church rather than as a mature commitment *to* the church. Based on her experience with sixth graders in a previous parish, Caroline Black says that parents often see confirmation as "a vaccination, a pill," that will somehow stamp their children "Episcopal," and so they encourage too-early confirmation.

Years ago I had a friend who wanted, as she put it, to "get my daughters done" before they stopped going to church. And yet confirmation is meant to be an adult choice, a personal—not a parental—decision. Mitchell writes that confirmation "is not appropriate for pre-adolescents" but he doesn't want to name a particular age because "people mature spiritually at different rates" (*What* 107). Black's experience is that traditional programs that simply stamp pre-adolescent young people with the ritual of confirmation don't "take." Young people who go through such programs are often among those who drop out.

Why, then, do such programs continue? Hartwell worries that clergy want to please the bishop by providing a reputable number of confirmands year by year; she suggests that some might be embarrassed if few or no confirmations took place during the bishop's annual visit. "It's a bishop issue" (though not of the bishops' making), she says of lock-step programs that confirm too young.

The Rev. Leslie Smith from Trinity Church, Princeton talks of having been "mildly skeptical" of their previous program. His parish undertook a two-year study of adolescent confirmation, after which they stopped routine confirmation and instead introduced Rite 13 and *Journey to Adulthood*. Trinity Church has been through two complete three year cycles of *Journey to Adulthood*, and Smith has found that the teenagers now "stay around the church." Of those older teenagers who elect to be confirmed, nearly all of them have been through *Journey to Adulthood* and have rich grounding in their faith. Smith meets regularly for a month or a month and a half with those seeking confirmation, then sits down one on one with each confirmand for several individual conversations. Smith comments that through family involvement, church involvement and the *Journey to Adulthood* program, these older teens come well prepared to make a mature decision about confirmation.

(For those who use the *Journey to Adulthood* program for ongoing youth ministry, we want to emphasize that *I will, with God's help* is not intended to replace *Journey*. *I will, with God's help* is designed as a short-term program that focuses on immediate preparation for the sacrament *only*, and can be used successfully whether or not your parish uses the full *Journey to Adulthood* program.)

The Rev. Justin Lindstrom, who runs the youth program at America's largest Episcopal parish, St. Martin's in Houston, says, "We don't want to confirm those who aren't serious." Confirmation, he says, is "not graduation" but integral to life in the church. Working with upwards of 90 teens at a time, Lindstrom says that St. Martin's confirmation program involves movement from whole group to small group activities, each small group consisting of 10-15 youth led by a mentor. Lindstrom also stresses that confirmation is the time when a person makes his or her decision for Christ: "In the Episcopal Church our confirmation is our altar call." With that theological understanding of confirmation (and despite the size of the confirmation classes), St. Martin's expects commitment from those participating—not just for the program, but for life.

This differs from the program Caroline Black described where the number of young confirmands was four times larger than regular Sunday School. "They came out of the woodwork" for the confirmation program because parents expected it—after which the youngsters considered themselves "done" with church-going and stopped attending.

Despite the low retention level of some early confirmation programs, Bishop Cadigan believes that such programs can be fruitful if they are part of ongoing family life within the church; confirmation is then part of the process of being a Christian, not a graduation from church life. He even suggests that a parent who isn't confirmed should join the program. (My husband and younger son attended classes and were confirmed together during Easter of 1991.)

In a very different setting, the Rev. Robert Jewett recently ran what he labeled a "Confirmation Conference" for seven young people in his rural Maine parish. Jewett agrees with Smith, Cadigan and Lindstrom that confirmation of teens needs to be part of continuous religious formation that goes on both at home and at church. All seven of this year's confirmands are active participants at St. Giles', and all come from families who are deeply involved in parish life. Because the confirmands are active teens from busy families, however, arranging time became an issue. Jewett ended up running his "Confirmation Conference" over three intensive days in August. Such an unusual program worked, he says, only because of who those particular young people were: confirmation was not their end-point, but a milestone on their journey in faith.

Another example of a confirmation program for committed teens was run by the Rev. Wendy Rozene, deacon at a suburban Episcopal parish. She co-taught a youth confirmation program that met on the first Sunday of the month between September and May. Most teens spent three years in the program before they felt ready for confirmation. Because the confirmation class also came to be their support system within the church, they stayed with it even after being confirmed, serving as mentors to the younger teens.

At the Church of the Holy Nativity, which meets in a converted auto parts store in the inner city of Baltimore, the Rev. Vicki Sirota also ran a confirmation program spanning three years. "Every year when I said, 'We're not ready yet,' it felt right." By the end of the third year, however, the confirmands finally felt prepared and "Mother Vicki" felt ready. What differed about her group of young people was family support: some had none. Instead the whole congregation acted as sponsoring guardians for those seeking confirmation. Despite lack of family, these young people have remained deeply committed to the church they have chosen. Across the street from the Church of the Holy Nativity drug dealers ply their trade; Sirota speaks of "spiritual warfare" in the neighborhood. Commitment to the church, therefore, becomes a serious choice, the church itself a refuge every time one makes it safely inside.

Around the country in these vastly different parishes, young people are making mature commitments to the church by renewing their Baptismal Covenant through confirmation. As family or parish involvement becomes integral, and as programs such as *Journey to Adulthood* or other long-term, experiential endeavors engage our youth, perhaps confirmation can become a serious *choice* rather than simply a "vaccination." UCLA researchers surveying nationwide college freshmen found that those who self-identified as Episcopalian or who listed Episcopal parents were "bright, articulate, and compassionate...more likely to participate in volunteer work"—and yet these bright, compassionate young adults "are leaving the Episcopal Church in higher percentages than in any other Christian denomination" (Easley 352).

How and when confirmation is "done" matters deeply. As things now stand, those who either go through confirmation too young or who do so simply because parents or parish expect it are likely to be lost to the Episcopal Church. Voicing concern for what becomes of those who do make a personal commitment to affirm their baptismal vows, Bishop Cadigan grieves the loss of college ministry, worrying about what happens to those energetic young people during the crucial years after they leave their home parish.

He is right to be concerned. As Ellen and Dana Charry remind us, "the world outside the church is often indifferent or hostile to Christian claims. Much of secular culture, which is ready to take hold of youth, is vulgar, violent and materialistic" (*Send* 709). In an extreme example, the Rev. Vicki Sirota daily encounters a vulgar, violent world that is eager to corrupt the neighborhood youth—and yet she says that even the drug dealers have an odd respect for the church as long as it is the church. (For this reason she refuses to carry a gun, refuses to buy into their vision of the world.)

At home, in the parish, on campus or in the inner city, the church needs to *be* the church, to be a beacon of hope and of love, to give people what Robert Sherman calls "a sense that reality is far greater than they imagine, that God is objectively real" and that, as Ellen Charry says, "God is committed to human flourishing" (*By* 37).

In other words, the Episcopal Church shouldn't run a "catch and release" program for its young people. Those parishes which offer confirmation to teens need to provide ongoing support and involvement. With that in place, young adult Episcopalians can be encouraged to claim their identity as deeply committed Christians.

Meanwhile, amidst all these legitimate concerns about confirmation programs for young people, over 19,000 adults are routinely confirmed in the Episcopal Church each year. Adults actually outnumber the younger confirmands. They come to an Inquirer's Class or confirmation program "really hungry," as Caroline Black notes, seeking understanding. Seeking a home parish. Seeking God. It is not just our youth, after all, who are bombarded by secular media and messages, but we adults, too, who live in "a world shorn of grace, mystery, compassion, and hope" (*By* 369).

By taking part in such a program, adults are witnesses to the mysterious grace of God which brought them there. Coming as they do in the midst of busy lives, adult participants are usually eager to wrestle like Jacob with what it means to be a beloved—though often wounded—child of God.

I will, with God's help is designed for those truly seeking to renew their Baptismal Covenant. The suggested activities are flexible enough to be used with adults, with youth or with intergenerational groups. These activities can:
- take place during a traditional six- to twelve-week program
- be condensed into an intensive Confirmation Conference
- be used from time to time over a three-year program.

Because the Baptismal Covenant is divided into six parts, there are six chapters devoted to the program. However, we encourage leaders to consider both prayerfully and creatively which activities best suit the needs of your participants.

PARISH INVOLVEMENT IN THE PROGRAM

Whether you use this program with adults, teens or a mix of both, be sure to solicit whole-parish involvement. This program should be as communal as Christianity itself. After all, "formation in Christian excellence is the responsibility of the Christian community" (By 52). The parish community should therefore be included.

On Sunday of the week when you will begin the program, be sure the service includes a prayer for the participants. Prayer #15, "For those about to be Baptized or to renew their Baptismal Covenant" on page 819 of *The Book of Common Prayer* would be particularly appropriate:

> *God, you prepared your disciples for the coming of the Spirit through the teaching of your Son Jesus Christ: Make the hearts and minds of your servants* (here you could name those who will be participating) *ready to receive the blessing of the Holy Spirit, that they may be filled with the strength of his presence; through Jesus Christ our Lord.* Amen.

Consider keeping this prayer as part of each Sunday service throughout the duration of the program (unless you will be spending three years as Wendy Rozene and Vicki Sirota have done—and then you might consider praying for participants once a month). For a group which includes those seeking confirmation, reception and reaffirmation, include all names equally.

The Rev. Lewis Sligh of Tampa suggests having participants in the program come forward during a Sunday service to sign their names in a special parish book. This, he says, hearkens back to the Book of Life in Revelation, and it recalls early centuries when Christians could be arrested for having their names in the book of believers. This public acknowledgment clearly signals the intention of those seeking to renew their Baptismal Covenant. The rest of the congregation, by witnessing this action, participate in it. (Sligh urges parish leaders to consider carefully what sort of book they would like to have for this ritual, since it will be something that the church maintains over the years.)

An even more important book is *The Book of Common Prayer*. We strongly recommend that the parish support those preparing to renew their Baptismal Covenant by giving a copy of *The Book of Common Prayer* to each participant *before* the program rather than at the end. Let each have a prayer book to peruse and to pray with during the program. The time they spend in this program may engage them more fully in the breadth and depth of the prayer book than any other time or circumstance in their lives. People build relationships with books as well as with one another. Your participants should have the chance to establish intimate connections with their own *Book of Common Prayer*.

Foster connections with parishioners, too. When Bob Jewett ran his Confirmation Conference, he circulated a sign-up sheet for people in the parish to provide snacks, fix lunches, take a photograph or come and witness. (Many others also suggested a group photograph taken early on and hung in a prominent place so that everyone in the parish could see those involved.) Jewett says the participants appreciated that members of the church community made time and effort to come and serve them.

During each of the sessions, a seasoned parishioner came and spoke about his or her experience with the church; Jewett felt it was important for the participants to hear these other witnesses, to know that "the church isn't just the person with a collar." Jewett also asked his participants in the program to interview two older parishioners to find out what being a member of St. Giles' meant to them.

Many parishes and programs also include mentors for small groups if the class is large, or even a separate mentor for each participant. Although not essential, the participation of mentors in *I will, with God's help* would be welcome: their stories, experiences and witness would enhance the various activities and discussions.

Perhaps the most touching story of parish involvement is Vicki Sirota's, whose entire congregation sponsored those confirmands with no family support. The parish still functions as the extended family for those young adults.

The Book of Common Prayer tells us that the "communion of saints is the whole family of God, the living and the dead, those whom we love and those whom we hurt, bound together in Christ by sacrament, prayer, and praise." Our congregations are outward and visible signs of that communion of saints. It is to this communion that your already-baptized participants belong, and to which they will be reaffirming their commitment as they renew their Baptismal Covenant. Find ways to remind the whole parish of their part in this program, from simple prayers to mentoring, from greeting the participants to sharing their stories—and by themselves taking part in the renewal of baptismal vows during the bishop's visit.

To prepare for each session, look through the list of what to bring and scan the "Session at a Glance" section near the beginning of each chapter. If time is short, pick and choose among the suggested activities. However, always include at least a short service from *The Book of Common Prayer*, a period of silence, a simple ritual and one or more of the activities. Encourage participants to use their journals; as Caroline Black points out, the interactive journals invite theological reflection—not so much "homework" as "Godwork."

A final note: my own prayers and blessings are with each of you as you take on leadership of this program. May it be well for you. May you feel God's grace and gratitude for the work you do. May you survive with a sense of humor, and a deeper sense of God.

I Believe: Living the Creed

PLAN THE SESSION

Celebrant: *Do you believe in God the Father?*

People: *I believe in God, the Father almighty, creator of heaven and earth.*

Celebrant: *Do you believe in Jesus Christ, the Son of God?*

People: *I believe in Jesus Christ, his only Son, our Lord.*
He was conceived by the power of the Holy Spirit and born of the Virgin Mary.
He suffered under Pontius Pilate, was crucified, died, and was buried.
He descended to the dead.
On the third day he rose again.
He ascended into heaven, and is seated at the right hand of the Father.
He will come again to judge the living and the dead.

Celebrant: *Do you believe in God the Holy Spirit?*

People: *I believe in the Holy Spirit, the holy catholic Church, the forgiveness of sins, the resurrection of the body, and the life everlasting.*

To Bring

- a floating candle (or a regular candle), a bowl for water and matches
- the opening line of a psalm, handwritten at the top of a piece of paper
- index cards
- copies of the Trinitarian intersecting circles (see p. 21)
- pens and pencils

- a Bible
- copies of *The Book of Common Prayer* (encourage participants to bring their own)
- copies of *The Hymnal 1982* (if closing with a hymn rather than a canticle)
- approximately twice as many stones as there are participants
- a watch or clock

Optional:
- a second bowl for water and either cloth or paper towels

Matters of Time

Single session: If you have a single session to cover this chapter, use as an opening service one of the appropriate short Daily Devotions beginning on page 137 in *The Book of Common Prayer.* Try not to feel rushed. Don't give up the brief period of silence which follows the communal psalm.

Two sessions: If you have two sessions for this chapter, spend the first introducing the community-building activities, the second more specifically on the creed. (Put that bluntly, it sounds appalling to "cover" what one believes about the Trinity in one or two weeks; clearly this is the work of a lifetime.) If you have two sessions, consider using one of the complete Morning, Noonday or Evening Prayer services in *The Book of Common Prayer* rather than the shorter devotions.

The Session(s) at a Glance

Gather

- select stones
- light the candle
- optional: "wash" stones
- set the stones
- compose the communal psalm
- share the appropriate service from *The Book of Common Prayer*
- read the psalm
- maintain short silence

Activities

- focus on the Apostles' Creed from Baptismal Covenant
- pass out journals

Closing

- pray for participants
- sing chosen hymn or recite chosen canticle
- retrieve stones
- exchange peace
- blow out candle

Leader's Reflection

The Baptismal Covenant, on which this program is based, begins with the Apostles' Creed: "I believe..." As you prepare for this first session, think about your own experience with both belief and doubt, with what has kept you not only in the Church, but willing to share your faith with this group of people who will soon become your own.

I'm reminded of the fox telling the Little Prince that we are responsible—forever—for what we have tamed. While you are neither "taming" nor even necessarily "training" the participants in your group, as you nurture their growth in faith and fellowship you will inevitably become part of one another's journeys. You will all become responsible one for the other.

Use the space below to record some of your most vivid memories of belief and doubt:

....

....

....

....

....

Of those memories, what do you feel most comfortable sharing with the participants in your program? What might be most helpful to people who are preparing to renew their Baptismal Covenants? What do you wish someone had shared with you when you undertook this same journey?

....

....

....

....

....

Be Tender to Yourself

Be sure to submit a prayer request asking the congregation to pray for you as well as for the participants in your program. (See the suggested prayer on page 15 of the Introduction.) Allow yourself to feel God's gratitude for this work you do. Remember that you are a child of God, infinitely loved and precious. No matter how each session goes, God is at work among you, and all will be well. Remember that you are working with people who have already been "sealed by the Holy Spirit in Baptism and marked as Christ's own forever," who are already part of your own extended family of Christians.

What are your biggest fears or biggest hopes as you face this opening session? Write them below, and offer them to God.

....

....

....

....

....

Before the Session

Note: The suggestions below look frighteningly long. That's because it's your *first* session. Experience suggests that the most awkwardness you're likely to encounter in leading a group would come during a first session, when you run out of activities, but have plenty of time left on the clock! You'll have more to prepare and plan for this session than for following ones, but nothing here is complicated. Really. Most of the suggestions are designed to get participants involved, to help you retreat to the background.

First pick an appropriate hymn or canticle for closing the sessions. Since I'm so tone deaf that my own children wouldn't let me sing lullabies, being asked to choose a hymn always terrifies me. The prayer book has a lovely and extensive selection of canticles, seven of them between pages 47 and 53, with fourteen more on pages 85-95. If you, too, are musically challenged, either ask another volunteer to lead the closing hymn
or pick a canticle to say rather than a hymn to sing.

Plan on using the same hymn or canticle for every session. This repetition helps establish a rhythm and ultimately a community.

Second prepare for the communal psalm that the participants will compose during this session by choosing a verse from a psalm and hand-writing it at the top of a piece of paper. If you can't think of a particular verse, some to consider include:

16:7   *I will bless the Lord who gives me counsel; my heart teaches me night after night.*

25:4   *Lead me in your truth and teach me, for you are the God of my salvation; in you have I trusted all the day long.*

42:1   *As the deer longs for the water-brooks, so longs my soul for you, O God.*

62:1   *For God alone my soul in silence waits; from the Lord comes my salvation.*

63:1   *O God, you are my God; eagerly I seek you; my soul thirsts for you, my flesh faints for you, as in a barren and dry land where there is no water.*

71:17   *O God, you have taught me since I was young, and to this day I tell of your wonderful works.*

What you will do during the actual session is to pass the paper on which you have written the verse to the person on your left. That person will then compose a verse to follow. When finished, he or she should fold the top of the paper over so the next participant can see only the newly written verse.

The paper will travel around the room, with each participant adding a single verse based just on the one preceding, folding it so only the new verse shows, and passing it on. In this way, each participant becomes co-author of the communal psalm.

If you have more than six participants, you might write the opening words of the psalm on separate pieces of paper so that no more than six people are working from one opening line. That way there isn't as much "dead time" for those not currently engaged in writing. Many psalms include repeated verses, so when you read the combined group effort during the session and later when you type it up, keep repeating the opening line just as it appears on the top of each paper.

Third photocopy the Trinitarian illustration for everyone.

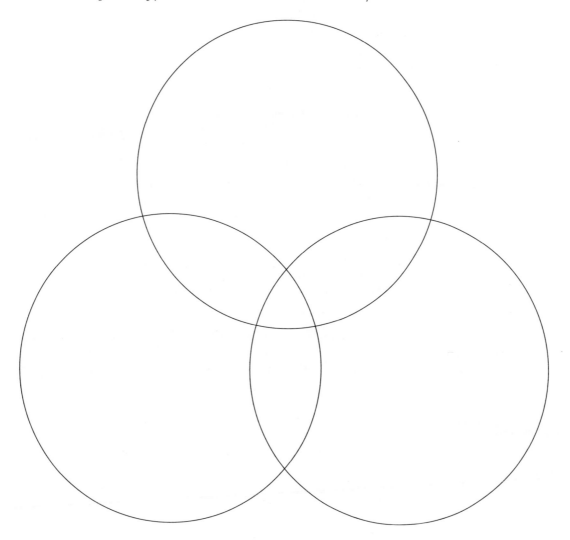

Before the participants arrive put a table in the middle of the room, and on it place a bowl of water, the floating candle (or a regular candle), a Bible and *The Book of Common Prayer*. This can be a big seminar table that everyone can fit around, or a small table just for this centering focus. Be sure to leave space around the candle for participants to place their stones. If you are willing to allow time for participants to "wash" the stones they select, set out the second bowl of water and towel(s).

Decide on the best place to lay out the collection of stones you bring. These can be stones you pick up on a walk, inexpensive pieces of gravel, polished stones from a craft store or river stones from a garden supply place. The river stones are my personal favorite: solid and satisfying to hold, these stones have come from water like the newly baptized.

Try to have almost twice as many stones as you need so that participants feel they have a real choice as they select a stone. This also gives you extras in case some participants forget to bring their stones to later sessions. Participants (including you) will use the stones to help "build the altar" at the beginning of each session, and to carry during the time between as tactile reminders of the journey they have chosen.

Group the chairs in a circle around the table. If participants don't yet have their own prayer books, set one on or beside each chair. If your parish has generously purchased prayer books for you to give each participant at the start of the program (which would be ideal), instead of setting them out ahead of time you may want to present the prayer books personally, either as part of the greeting or just prior to the service.

Note: Having coffee, tea, soft drinks or even water available at each session would be a hospitable touch, but if preparing and cleaning up for this feels like one more thing in your already busy schedule, don't do it. The next chapter on Teaching, Fellowship, Bread and Prayer does ask that you bring bread, but at other sessions food or drink is entirely up to you. (Providing such items could be part of wider parish involvement.)

If you are including, as Bishop Knudsen and others strongly urge, a service component as part of the preparation for renewing baptismal vows, you will need to make arrangements ahead of time with local agencies so that each participant will have the chance to perform authentic service within the wider community. This might be a place to enlist advice and help from parishioners already involved in social action or peace and justice. (Try to involve others in the parish as much as possible; you really don't have to do everything on your own.)

THE SESSION

Gather

As participants arrive, greet them individually. Once everyone is there, welcome them to this program, and ask them each to select a stone from the collection you brought. Explain that they will then place their stones around the lighted candle as a way to help "build" an altar at the beginning of each session. Between sessions, they can either carry the stone with them or put it in a prominent place, whichever will serve best to remind them of their commitment to this journey.

Share with them some of the ancient history of stones in scripture, from the stone altars Abraham built, to the stone pillow on which Jacob slept when he dreamed of the ladder between earth and heaven, to Jesus as the cornerstone of the Church. If participants have seen *Schindler's List*, they will have seen the survivors placing stones (not flowers) on Oskar Schindler's grave; even now in Jewish cemeteries from Jerusalem to Trevose, Pennsylvania, people bring stones to place on the graves of loved ones. Suggest that they look closely at their stones so they will be able to recognize them when they retrieve them at the end of the session.

Once each participant has selected a stone, it's your turn to choose one. After doing so, light the floating candle and place it in the bowl of water. Remind participants that what they are preparing for—whether it's confirmation, reception or reaffirmation—is the renewal of their Baptismal Covenant, and baptism is a sacrament involving water. Use the first part of the "Thanksgiving over the Water at Baptism," from page 306 in the prayer book:

> *We thank you, Almighty God, for the gift of water. Over it the Holy Spirit moved in the beginning of creation. Through it you led the children of Israel out of their bondage in Egypt into the land of promise. In it your Son Jesus received the baptism of John and was anointed by the Holy Spirit as the Messiah, the Christ, to lead us, through his death and resurrection, from the bondage of sin into everlasting life.*

> *We thank you, Father, for the water of Baptism. In it we are buried with Christ in his death. By it we share in his resurrection. Through it we are reborn by the Holy Spirit.*

Remind participants that each of them has already been baptized and reborn in the name of the Father, and of the Son, and of the Holy Spirit. Each is already a stone in the foundation of faith, a living member of the Church, part of the Body of Christ. What they are doing in this program is preparing to *renew* the Baptismal Covenant. Baptism itself is forever. They are already children of God, full members of the household of faith.

Optional: If you brought the extra bowl of water and towels, this would be the appropriate time to invite participants to come forward one at a time and symbolically "wash" their chosen stones, immersing the stones in the second bowl of water and drying them on the towel(s). This activity not only reminds them of the waters of baptism; it also allows them to become more familiar with their stones so that they can reclaim them at the end of this (and every) session. Once everyone is done, proceed to the next step.

Invite each participant now to step forward, clearly say the name by which he or she was baptized, and place each stone on the table around the candle. Model this for them by doing it first, being sure to articulate your name clearly. Once you have placed your stone, step back into the circle. Listen carefully as each participant speaks his or her name, holding each in prayer.

Once everyone is finished, sit down. Explain that they are now going to compose a communal psalm. Show them that you have written a verse from a psalm at the top of a piece of paper, and explain the procedure for completing the task. Circulate the page(s). Encourage honesty and spontaneity; no one should ponder for too long.

Having participated in this activity on separate retreats with adults and with teenagers as well as in a mixed-age Christian creative writing class, I remain awed that it works so well. If anyone is stumped or scared, remind them of Jesus' words not to worry about what to say; the Spirit will speak for them. You might also mention that some verses in the psalms are very, very short, and that's ok, too.

Once everyone has written, read their communal psalm aloud. Tell the participants that you will make copies for each of them to have for the following sessions. Congratulate them.

Now lead the participants in whichever service you have selected from *The Book of Common Prayer*. (Omit the Lord's Prayer since you will pray it after the brief period of silence.)

Once the service is over, tell them that you will read their psalm aloud one more time, and that afterwards there will be a brief period of silence. Suggest that they find a comfortable position in their chairs, that they breathe deeply, and that during the silence they focus on a line from the psalm, on the name of Jesus or on their own rhythmic breathing. Encourage them simply to rest in the presence of God.

Suggest that they close their eyes and begin conscious breathing as you read their communal psalm to them again. Then time the silence. It's easy to quit too soon; be sure to allow *at least two full minutes*. End the silence by praying the Lord's Prayer together.

Note: If you plan two sessions on this chapter, skip ahead to the Closing: pass out journals, sing or recite the chosen hymn or canticle, have each participant retrieve his or her stone and exchange the peace. At the next session, set up the table as before. (You may switch to a conventional rather than a floating candle from now on if you like.) Then place the stones, share the communal psalm (pass out copies if you have had time to prepare them), observe a period of silence and conduct the chosen service before going on to "I Believe."

Focus: *I Believe*

One of my seminary professors, Robert Sherman, bluntly states, "God is as real as gravity." God isn't some esoteric philosophical idea, but is instead the most deeply grounded, absolute, objective Reality. We don't have to "believe in" God for God to exist.

God is. As Karl Barth explains, "*credo ut intelligam*, 'I believe in order to understand'" (*Evangelical Theology* 44)—not the reverse.

The Apostles' Creed, which forms the basis of our Baptismal Covenant, is the Church's ancient statement of belief. Both Morning and Evening Prayer services include the Apostles' Creed. Those who follow the daily offices are thereby embraced by this reminder of their deepest identity as Christians, people who have been "sealed by the Holy Spirit in Baptism and marked as Christ's own forever." Morning and evening, they focus on their faith and the Baptismal Covenant they will now renew in the sacrament of confirmation.

The creed is not so much a dogmatic formula which Christians must sign before entry into the Church as it is what Johnston calls "a summary of the community story" into which the newly baptized are welcomed (15). Participants in this program have already been baptized, already welcomed, already embraced as full members of the community of faith. They should, although some may not, already be familiar with the stories which shape the Church and which inform the creed. The Apostles' Creed contains an outline—a table of contents, if you will—of those stories.

Ask the participants to turn to page 304 in the prayer book and actually read through the whole Baptismal Covenant with them, taking the role of celebrant. Once again stress that this covenant is the core of their preparation for confirmation, reception or reaffirmation. They are already under this covenant, full members of the Church. What this program hopes to do is to help participants define more clearly what it means to be a baptized Christian, what it means to be in a covenant relationship with God, what they mean when they say, "I believe...."

The word "creed" comes from the Latin word *credere*, which translates as "what I put my heart (or my trust) in." Pass out index cards to the participants and ask them to take about 3 minutes to write a personal creed: what they put their heart, their trust in. Share an example from your own experience. What are those things that draw your heart and your trust?

....

....

....

....

....

Ask participants to share what they wrote. Be willing to start with your own list of what draws your heart and your trust.

Once you have spent some time on this, point out that a creed is a kind of "mission statement." Their personal creeds should function as a kind of road map of their direction in life. Tell participants that the opening of the Baptismal Covenant is actually the Apostles' Creed, the ancient, foundational statement of Christian believing, the road map for Christians.

Show participants the Outline of Faith ("commonly called the Catechism") beginning on page 845 at the back of the prayer book, which is essentially an extended commentary on the creeds. You may, as the rubrics suggest, pray with some of these questions and answers —not "study" or memorize them, as in past generations, but *pray* with them during the course of this program.

During this session you will pray with four of the segments. Begin with "The Creeds," and then follow with "God the Father," "God the Son" and "The Holy Spirit." (Should any be interested, the Athenasian Creed is included with historical documents on page 864.) Before you begin, ask participants to take a few deep breaths, to enter into a meditative state and to pray their responses as they speak them.

Pray "The Creeds" (page 851) and then move expeditiously to "God the Father" (page 846). After those questions, and before moving on to "God the Son," recite the following prayer:

> *I will give thanks unto thee, for I am fearfully and wonderfully made: marvelous are thy works, and that my soul knoweth right well... My God and my All, my beginning and my end, My sole and everlasting good, My God and my All. Amen. (Farrer 32)*

Then move to "God the Son" (page 849). After praying those questions and answers, and before moving on to "The Holy Spirit," recite the following prayer:

> *Lord Jesus, stay with us; be our companion in the way, kindle our hearts and awaken hope, that we may know you as you are revealed in Scripture and the breaking of bread. Grant this for the sake of your love. Amen.*

Then move to "The Holy Spirit" on page 852. After those questions and answers, pray the following Orthodox prayer to the Holy Spirit. You might suggest that participants close their eyes as you pray:

> *Serene Light, shining in the ground of my being: Draw me to yourself; draw me past the snares of the senses, out of the mazes of the mind. Free me from symbols, words, that I may discover the Signified, the Word unspoken, in the darkness that veils the ground of my being. Amen.*

As participants put away prayer books, quote Julian of Norwich's words: "God stands nearer to us than our own souls, for he is the ground on which we stand" (161).

Point out that the creed, like the Trinity to whom they have just prayed, is in three parts. As the Rev. Dan Warren from St. Paul's, Brunswick, Maine notes, as human beings, we are embedded in trinities. Ask participants to think for a moment about what three things give balance and stability to their lives. Pass out the paper with the three intersecting circles. Point out that the center—the place where the three circles all intersect—makes a triangle. Ask them to write their name in that central place, to represent their core self. Then they should fill each circle with one of the three things which give the most balance, stability and strength to their lives

Think about your own life: what three things are primary in terms of commitment, balance, passion? At the most basic level, most of us live in the trinity of self, family and job or school. One woman listed her trinity as: writing, relationships, God. A teen listed: friends, music, food. What is your trinity?

....

....

....

....

....

After a brief time to ponder, ask participants to share their trinitarian balancing acts. How many had a hard time limiting their list to three? (Did you?) What does that say about the busyness of our lives? Ask them to reflect back on their personal creeds. Where are the overlaps between their creeds and their personal trinities? If there are none, should there be?

As you finish out this portion of the session, use the following prayer:

> *God above me, Father from whence my being descends, on whom my existence hangs, to whom I turn up my face, to whom I stretch out my hands:*
>
> *God beside me, God in a [hu]man like me, Jesus Christ in the world with me, whose hand lays hold of me, presenting me, with yourself, to God:*
>
> *God within me, soul of my soul, root of my will, inexhaustible fountain, Holy [Spirit]:*
>
> *Threefold Love, one in yourself, unite your forces in me, come together in the citadel of my conquered heart.*
>
> *You have loved me with everlasting love. Teach me to care. Amen (Farrer 23).*

Focus: Journals

Pass out journals. Read through the whole opening page with them (reprinted below):

My baptismal name is _____

I was sealed by the Holy Spirit in baptism and marked as Christ's own forever

on _____ .

My sponsors/godparents were _____

I want to join in this program so that I can renew my baptismal vows. The Baptismal Covenant describes both Christian belief and Christian responsibility. By beginning this journey, I am making a mature commitment to God and to the Church.

Signature: _____

Witness: _____

Date: _____

Ask participants to write their baptismal name. Ask how many actually know the date of their baptism—and encourage those who don't to find out. Read slowly through the statement which they will sign indicating their intention to participate in this program leading to a renewal of their baptismal vows. Go around and sign as "witness." (If you have a large group that breaks into smaller groups, do this in the smaller groups, asking the group leaders or mentors to sign as witnesses.)

Then have participants turn to the next page where it says "Always remember" and in that space ask them to write as you dictate Paul's words to the Romans (8:38-39):

> *For I am sure that neither death, nor life, nor angels, nor principalities, nor things present, nor things to come, nor powers, nor height, nor depth, nor anything else in all creation, will be able to separate us from the love of God in Christ Jesus our Lord.*

Tell them to turn to these words when discouraged or troubled in any way. Stress that *nothing* can ever separate them from God's love. Nothing. They have all been sealed by the Holy Spirit in baptism and marked as Christ's own forever. Suggest that they copy these words onto a note card that they can carry in their wallets—someplace easily and always available should they need reminding of God's eternal love for them.

Point out those pages in the journal that you would like to have them encounter before the next session. (Note that beginning after the next session they will be praying for one another. This time they should pray for themselves as they begin their journey.) Give them time to flip through pages just to get a feel for the kinds of responses the journal asks of them.

Make them aware of the pages set aside for reflecting on sermons they hear during the course of their preparation. Show them the section devoted to Luke, which they will begin after the next session, and encourage them to begin thinking about their spiritual journey, written about in the final pages in their journal. Then ask them to put the journals aside and prepare for closing exercises.

If you are including a service component, this would be an appropriate time to discuss how and when it will begin, with whom they will be working and what the expectations will be. Remind them of the title of this program, the responses made to the baptismal covenant: *I will, with God's help.* The service they will do is part of their Baptismal Covenant.

Finally, ask participants to bring advertisements from magazines, newspapers and junk mail to the next session. Explain that together you will look at ways society tries to shape our beliefs.

Closing

Close this session with the prayer "For those about to be baptized or to renew their Baptismal Covenant" from page 819 of the prayer book:

O God, you prepared your disciples for the coming of your Spirit through the teaching of your Son Jesus Christ: Make the hearts and minds of your servants* _____ ready to receive the blessing of the Holy Spirit, that they may be filled with his presence; through Jesus Christ our Lord. Amen.

(*If you have a fairly small group, name each participant here.)

Ask them to turn to the hymn or canticle that you will be using at the end of each session. Then stand up and sing the hymn or read the canticle together.

Invite participants to retrieve their chosen stones, then step back into the circle.

Exchange the peace:

Leader:　　　The peace of the Lord be always with you.
Participants:　And also with you.

Blow out the candle.

After the Session

Looking Back, Looking Forward

Once all the participants have left, allow yourself a brief moment of reflection.

Where did you particularly feel God's grace among you during this session?

....

....

....

....

....

....

What do you wish had happened that didn't—or what did happen that you wish hadn't?

....

....

....

....

....

....

Offer it all to God, both the gracious and the grueling.

Be open to feel God's gratitude for your time and for your caring.

Go in peace, knowing that you have served God well.

Teaching, Fellowship, Bread and Prayers

PLAN THE SESSION

Celebrant: *"Will you continue in the apostles' teaching and fellowship, in the breaking of bread, and in the prayers?"*

People: *"I will, with God's help."*

To Bring

- a candle and matches
- the communal psalm composed at the first session
- advertisements from magazines, newspapers and junk mail
- index cards
- pens and pencils
- extra Bibles
- prayer books (encourage participants to bring their own)
- the left-over stones from the first session
- a watch (if no clock is visible)
- bread to share

Optional:
- Gospel films: *Jesus of Nazareth*, directed by Franco Zeffirelli; *The Gospel According to Saint Matthew*, directed by Pier Paolo Pasolini (black and white with subtitles); *A Dramatic Presentation of the Gospel of Mark* by David Rhoads; or even *Jesus Christ Superstar* or *Godspell.*
- bread-based items for pot luck (such as bagels or sweet rolls for breakfast, sandwiches or pizza for lunch or supper)
- butter, cream cheese or peanut butter
- napkins or paper towels

Matters of Time

Single session: This question in the Baptismal Covenant embraces the whole formation of Christian identity. If you have only a single session to cover this chapter, use as your service the appropriate short Daily Devotions beginning on page 137 in *The Book of Common Prayer,* and assign more of Luke to be read at home, reminding the participants that reading scripture is always a communal act, even when done in solitude. *Do not give up the brief period of silence. Do not feel rushed.* Omit all the optional items.

Two sessions: If you have two sessions for this chapter, spend the first on "teaching and fellowship," and the second on "bread and prayer." Wait for the second session to bring the optional items. Consider using one of the complete Morning, Noonday or Evening Prayer services in *The Book of Common Prayer.*

Longer/retreat session: The material in this chapter could also be done in a day-long (or overnight) retreat, with all of Luke read aloud, built-in time for contemplative prayer, longer story-telling sessions, one of the suggested films and several shared meals. In such a setting, it would be appropriate to gather throughout the day for Morning, Noonday and Evening Prayer services.

If a "movie session" seems feasible (for you as well as for the participants), but doesn't fit into a weekend schedule, the movie(s) could be shown at a separate time and place, with snacks during the movie and conversation afterwards to consider what this particular telling of the story says about Jesus Christ.

The Session(s) at a Glance

Gather
- light the candle
- set the stones
- read together the communal psalm
- maintain short silence
- share the appropriate service from *The Book of Common Prayer*

Activities
- focus on apostles' teaching:
  — explore the Apostles' Creed
  — begin Luke
  — optional: In a longer/retreat setting, this would also be the appropriate time for the film.
- focus on fellowship:
  — community-building through story-telling
  — prayer cards
  — optional: retreat suggestions

- focus on breaking bread:
  — share the bread (If you are sharing a pot luck bread-based meal, this would be the time for it.)
  — bread of scripture
- focus on prayer:
  — overview of *The Book of Common Prayer*

Closing

- sing chosen hymn or recite chosen canticle
- retrieve stones
- remind group members to use their journals between sessions
- exchange peace
- blow out candle

Leader's Reflection

In the Australian prayer book, just before the blessing at the end of Confirmation, comes this injunction: "All who have been baptized and confirmed are called to study the Bible, to take part in the life of the Church, to share in the Holy Communion and to pray faithfully and regularly" (93).

This is the answer to today's question from the Baptismal Covenant: "Will you continue in the apostles' teaching and fellowship, in the breaking of bread, and in the prayers?" This is what each baptized Christian is called to do, with God's help.

As you prepare to present this chapter, consider your own experiences. What are some of your most vivid memories, some of your most important moments of Christian study, fellowship, Eucharist and prayer?

....

....

....

....

Of those memories and moments, what do you feel most compelled to share with the participants in your program? What would be most helpful as you direct them to consider their own Christian formation? What do you wish someone had told you?

....

....

....

....

Be Tender to Yourself

Continue to ask the congregation's prayers for yourself as well as for the participants in your program, and allow yourself to feel God's gratitude for this work you do. Remember that you are a child of God, infinitely loved and precious. No matter how each session goes, God is at work among you all, and all will be well.

What are your biggest fears or biggest hopes for this session? Write them below, and offer them to God.

....

....

....

....

....

Before the Session

In the space on the next page, copy down or tape to the page the communal psalm that the participants composed at the first session. Sometime during the week, type up this psalm and print or photocopy enough for the group. (If you have no time for making copies, you can simply read your handwritten version at the appropriate time. The best option, of course, would be to enlist help from a member of the parish for the typing and photocopying.)

Based on how often you are meeting, determine how many chapters of Luke participants should read between each session. Since Luke has 24 chapters, if you have only four more meetings after this one, that would balance out to six chapters between sessions. With eight more meetings, participants would need to read three chapters between the sessions.

Before the participants arrive put a table in the middle of the room. On the table, place a candle, a Bible, *The Book of Common Prayer* and whatever bread you brought. As in the first session(s), this can be a big seminar table that everyone can fit around, or a small table just for this centering focus. Be sure to leave space around the candle for participants to place the stones they chose at the first session. (If some have forgotten or lost their stones, let them choose new ones from the leftovers.)

Have chairs grouped around the table. If participants don't have their own copies of *The Book of Common Prayer*, place one on or beside each chair.

Communal Psalm

THE SESSION

Gather

Once everyone has arrived, gather in a circle around the table. Tell the participants that once you have lit the candle, they should step forward one at a time to place their stones around it, speaking their names as they do so. After you light the candle, place your own stone nearby on the table, say your name, then step back.

Once the participants have all arranged their stones and named themselves, ask them to sit down while you pass out copies of the communal psalm they composed. Explain that just as they brought their separate stones to help "build" the altar, so they brought their own words to help write this psalm. Tell them that once you have all read the psalm in unison, there will be a brief period of silence (2-5 minutes, depending on what feels comfortable to you as you continue to assess your group). Ask them to find a comfortable position in their chairs and to breathe deeply. During the silence, they can focus on a line from the psalm, on the name of Jesus or on their own rhythmic breathing. Encourage them simply to rest in the presence of God.

Remaining seated, lead the participants in reciting their psalm, or read the psalm aloud to them, if you have only one copy. Then time the silence; it's easy to quit too soon, so be sure to allow *at least two full minutes*.

End the silence by praying the Lord's Prayer together. Then lead the group in whatever service you have selected ahead of time from *The Book of Common Prayer*.

Focus: The Apostles' Teaching

Explore the Creed

In ancient Hebrew and early Christian culture, communal reading of scripture was a shared experience, a joyful encounter with the Living God. Roger Ferlo says that after the Reformation, Christian reading of scripture became less playful, more "individualistic and isolating" (72). This is your chance to bring some of that joy back, to make the Bible more user-friendly, accessible and inviting for your participants.

After the service, ask participants to turn to page 304 in the prayer book and point out the question for this session. Read it to them, having them give the appropriate response:

> *Leader:* Will you continue in the apostles' teaching and fellowship, in the breaking of bread, and in the prayers?
>
> *Participants:* I will, with God's help.

Point out that the Apostles' Creed, which they examined last time, actually summarizes the apostles' teaching. Read them once again the question and answer from page 852 in the Catechism regarding the Apostles' Creed:

Q: What is the Apostles' Creed?

A: The Apostles' Creed is the ancient creed of Baptism; it is used in the Church's daily worship to recall our Baptismal Covenant.

At this point, divide participants into pairs. Ask each pair of participants to use page 304 again to ask each other the questions regarding the creed, taking turns as questioner and answerer. Besides serving to review last week's focus on the creed, this invites each participant to articulate the creed.

Next ask the pairs to consider the voices in our contemporary materialistic culture that try to tell us *other things* in which to believe. Quote Karl Barth's awareness that "the voice of the old serpent" can call the community away from the Christian story to "all sorts of strange voices" (*Evangelical Theology* 45). To give a sense of what those other voices might be, read them the following "thanksgiving prayer" recorded by Michael Johnston:

> *We give thanks to you, O God, for the goodness and love which you have made known to us in Hollywood; for money and power and popularity, for good looks, hard bodies, blond hair, and straight teeth; for the word spoken by People magazine; for happy endings (13).*

If participants brought along advertisements or other examples of contemporary attempts to shape our "beliefs," ask them to look at these now. Give each pair an index card and a pen or pencil, and ask them to take 5 minutes and write a secular, materialistic creed based on contemporary American culture. Emphasize that you want them to write *not* a creed that they actually believe in, but one that *our culture tells us to believe in*.

Explain that, as with their communal psalm, you will gather all their ideas and type their version of a contemporary secular creed and then bring it back for the session on "Proclaiming the Good News by Word and Example." Ask each pair to begin its work by writing either "I believe ..." or "My culture tells me to believe..." on their index cards. During the 5 minutes the participants work, use the space below to list ideas of your own about what our culture lures us to believe in:

....

....

....

....

....

After 5 minutes, ask group members to share what they came up with. Share your ideas as well. (Remember to collect their index cards so you have them for the session "By Word and Example.")

After you finish talking about the secular beliefs that surround us, tell them that contemporary theologians over and over emphasize the need to recognize—in order to turn away from—these voices and creeds of contemporary culture which seek to lure us from love of God to other loves and longings. We can laugh at our awareness, but we need to take seriously that what we are about as Christians is counter-cultural, a turning from the glitter of worldly goods to the still small voice of the Spirit, the companionship of Jesus Christ, the steadfast love of God.

As Johnston says, despite Madison Avenue's desire to be our source of truth and beauty, the Bible in fact "is the collection of texts that assembles the [Christian] community and against which all other communities and stories are measured....they are the stories of the family and the community to which we belong. They make sense out of our lives, our relationships, our world and our God. They are our true stories" (18/23). It is the stories gathered in scripture that tell us who we are.

We need to know those stories. Julia Easley asks, "How many of us know the stories in Scripture, the family tales of our faith community, as well as we know the stories about Aunt Helen or Grandpa Gene, the tales of our birth families?" (353). Many of us don't. All of us should.

Begin Luke

At this point, remind the participants that as part of this program they will actually read one of the community's most beloved stories in its entirety: the Gospel according to Luke. (Their journals provide space for responding.) By way of introduction, ask them to turn to one of the last events in Luke, the tale of weary travelers on the road to Emmaus, Luke 24:13-35.

This is a narrative of well-meaning people who thought they got the story wrong, but who, through examination of scripture—through *teaching*—were ultimately able to recognize Jesus in the breaking of bread. Share the reading, asking each person to read one or two verses, pausing after each reader (except the last) to answer questions or make commentary.

Without commentary after the last verse, simply read "A Collect for the Presence of Christ" found on page 124 in *The Book of Common Prayer*. (If you meet in the morning, omit the phrase "for evening is at hand and the day is past.")

Lord Jesus, stay with us, for evening is at hand and the day is past; be our companion in the way, kindle our hearts, and awaken hope, that we may know you as you are revealed in Scripture and the breaking of bread. Grant this for the sake of your love. Amen.

Point out that Jesus invited the travelers into the stories of scripture *before* breaking bread with them. Remind them that in the service for Holy Eucharist we read scripture first (usually three lessons and a psalm) *before* we approach the table for communion.

Reiterate: Know the stories, the collective teachings of the Church. Then, in Christian fellowship, break bread together.

Remind the participants that they should begin reading the Gospel according to Luke before the next session, keeping track in the Notes and Quotes section of their journals. Provide guidelines for how many chapters they should read between sessions. If you have time, you could read and reflect on the first chapter together. If you are covering all of "Teaching, Fellowship, Bread and Prayer" in a single session, move more expeditiously on to "Fellowship."

Optional: Show a Film

If time allows (in a longer session or retreat day), this would be when you might consider showing one of the films, followed by discussion of how the director chose to tell the story of Jesus' life, death and resurrection.

When I was in seminary, the Rev. Kathy Grieb invited her "Gospel of God" class to an optional Saturday of four "Jesus movies," including afternoon showings of *The Last Temptation of Christ* and Monty Python's *Life of Brian*. Several of my classmates left in the afternoon, too deeply disturbed by one or the other of those two films to sit through them. Disturbing they may be, but for those who stayed, the films sparked thoughtful conversation about how we see—and inwardly digest—the gospel stories.

Be sensitive to the ages and sensibilities of your group before undertaking such an exhaustive and exhausting endeavor, however. For those who have read and "inwardly digested" the gospel stories, film re-tellings that violate their interpretations may literally make them feel sick, as though they have taken in something indigestible. For those with limited background in scripture, one of the traditional interpretations would be a more appropriate starting place. The original film suggestions offer plenty to ponder.

Focus: Fellowship

Storytelling

Christianity, William Willimon says, "is not a home correspondence course in salvation. This religion is anything but a private affair" (21). Over and over again we are reminded that there is no such thing as a solitary Christian. We are all adopted sons and daughters of God, brothers and sisters of our Lord Jesus Christ. We begin the Lord's Prayer with "Our Father"—not mine alone, but yours as well; "the God and Father of all." We are part of the whole Christian family. "Whether I want it or not," writes Roberta Bondi, "the fact is that whenever I speak these words, '*our* Father...give *us...our* daily bread,' by virtue of my very baptism I am praying it as part of the people of God, and in return they are praying it with me" (26).

Most of the time we forget our connectedness, but once as I stood alone on a desert hill in Arizona watching the scarlet sunset, I suddenly felt surrounded by clouds of witnesses, hearing their voices singing down the centuries: "O gracious light, pure brightness of the everliving Father in heaven, O Jesus Christ, holy and blessed..." The Rev. Lewis Sligh once spoke of an Easter service in which he sensed the heavens open, and at an intimate, soul level he understood what it means to be part of the communion of saints.

Our connection to others not only involves those we encounter daily, those in any need or trouble, those we love and those we hurt, but it also includes those who have gone before us. Americans are trained to believe in rugged, independent individualism. Christianity, on the other hand, calls us to community, to interdependence, to fellowship. Christianity, remember, is a counter-cultural affair.

To help share this insight on Christian fellowship with the participants, remind them of those communal words of the Lord's Prayer. Remind them that, as baptized Christians, they are "very members incorporate" in the family of Jesus Christ. Explain that as a way of building a sense of community, you are going to ask each participant not only to say his or her name again, but to tell a brief story that says something about the teller.

Admit that this can be hard for some. Even Roberta Bondi, accustomed to giving public addresses, admitted to fear and panic when asked to share her own story the first time. After having done so, however, she was deeply aware of God's grace: "I found myself looking through the transparent colors of the story of my chipped and jagged life, and the light of that same, mysterious saving holy beauty was pouring through it" (46). Our lives *are* chipped and jagged, but it is from such brokenness that mosaics or stained glass windows are made, the pattern beautiful, the image made whole from all the broken pieces. The pieces of our collective stories, after all, make up the Body of Christ.

Then begin this story-sharing activity by stating your name and telling one very short story about yourself—anything from a childhood memory to a current joy or grief, from showing yourself to be clumsy at sports or good at math, a loving parent or an absent-minded friend. Keep it simple but specific.

Moving to the left, ask each participant to say his or her name and tell a brief personal story. When everyone is finished, remind them that what they just heard were family stories, brought to this gathering like their stones, taken from pockets in the mind and set down in front of everyone. Each story is now part of the whole gathering, part of the body of Christ.

Encourage them to understand that being part of the body of Christ is more than metaphor. As Marianne Micks says, "Christians really are the hands and feet of the post-Easter Jesus....You and I are the soft connective tissue which holds Christ's body together" (61).

Prayer Cards

To reinforce the communal nature of Christian fellowship, the participants will be responsible for praying for one another during the time between meetings. Pass out note cards and ask them to print their names clearly. Collect the cards, shuffle them and then randomly pass them out. If some end up with their own names, ask them to trade.

Invite the group members to look in their journals for the place to enter the person's name, and to be faithful about praying for this person every day. Ask them not to lose the card but to bring it back to the next session.

Optional: Retreat Suggestions

Another way for people to encounter Christian fellowship is through retreat time, not just with this group but at a retreat center such as an Episcopal convent or monastery, or, for older teens, at state-wide events such as Happenings or Teens Encountering Christ. This kind of experience with other Christians lets the participants know how deeply real God is; it lets them live for a brief time in the counter-cultural world of Christianity, away from the pull of daily life.

This would be a good time to suggest such a retreat and to come armed with a list of possibilities. "Communal practices," writes Ellen Charry in *By the Renewing of Your Minds*, "such as participation in prayer, liturgy, sacraments, and study all strengthen Christian identity" (27). Some parishes actually require a retreat experience as part of the preparation for confirmation.

As a segue into the Breaking of Bread, remind your participants that fellowship often involves food.

Note: If you are covering this chapter in two sessions, close this gathering with the chosen hymn or canticle. Ask each participant to retrieve his or her own stone, and remind them to pray for one another. Say that you you will pray for all of them, and ask their prayers for you. End with an exchange of the peace. When you return for the second session connected to this chapter, set up the table as before, this time with the bread as well. Follow steps for placing stones, reading the psalm, keeping silence and praying a service before going on to Breaking the Bread.

Focus: Breaking the Bread

Sharing Bread

Jesus kept getting in trouble with the Pharisees because of his table fellowship with sinners. But he kept on sitting down with them. (This is a good thing for us sinners.)

Later, when Peter found himself questioning Paul's inclusion of gentiles at the Lord's Table, God sent him a vision so that he might know "that I should not call any man common or unclean." As baptized Christians gather at the Eucharist, there is, as Paul tells us, neither slave nor free, neither Jew nor Greek, neither male nor female, but all equally welcome members of the family of Jesus Christ The sacraments, like other aspects of Christian life, are communal:"There are no solo sacraments," as Barbara Brown Taylor reminds us in *The Preaching Life* (66). We're in this together.

Breaking bread together, whether at the Eucharist or at the kitchen table, is a bonding experience. The word "companion" actually comes from the Latin *cum*, meaning "with," and *panis*, meaning "bread." In other words, companions are those with whom we break bread. Sharing food is one of life's most intimate activities, a necessary element of Christian fellowship. Prepare by considering some of your own memories of meals:

....

....

....

....

....

For this part of the session, tell participants the meaning of "companion," then simply say a brief thanksgiving—"Bless, O Lord, this bread to our use and us to your service"—and break the bread.

Try to make this an informal time to eat, talk and relax into knowing that "when two or three are gathered" in the name of Jesus Christ, he's there. He's with you.

A question you might ask during this time, if it feels appropriate, is what group members carry as a dominant memory of the Eucharist. (Be willing to share your own, especially since some of your group may not have such memories.) An easier question, and one which everyone should be able to answer, would ask for the memory of a particular meal, such as Thanksgiving. Ask:
- What made it memorable?
- Who was there?
- Was it the food or the companionship or the event surrounding the meal that made it memorable?

Perhaps after this discussion, you could bring in the Eucharist if it didn't seem right before.

Bread of Scripture

As you near the end of this Breaking the Bread segment of the session, one way of looking back to the apostles' teaching as well as looking ahead toward Prayers would be to talk briefly about the connection between reading scripture and eating nourishing food. Remind them of such common phrases as "devouring a good book." Quote Jeremiah:

Your words were found, and I ate them, and your words became to me a joy and the delight of my heart.

Read them the collect for the Sunday closest to Nov. 16 (written by Thomas Cranmer for the 1559 prayer book, found on page 184 and 236 of our current *Book of Common Prayer*):

Blessed Lord, who has caused all holy Scriptures to be written for our learning: Grant us so to hear them, read, mark, learn, and inwardly digest them, that we may embrace and ever hold fast the blessed hope of everlasting life, which you have given us in our Savior Jesus Christ; who lives and reigns with you and the Holy Spirit, one God, for ever and ever. Amen.

If you haven't done so before, this might be a time to discuss how a deep devouring of scripture, this inward digesting of stories in the Bible, feeds us, nourishes us. As Ferlo says, "Communion with God is made possible by tasting the sacred page. Reading the Bible offers a contact with God's Word as immediate and intimate as eating" (11). Invite participants to share memories of reading that felt, to them, as satisfying as eating good food. Ask them to discuss times and ways when reading the Bible might be the nourishment they need most.

Close out this portion of the session by singing (or saying) just the opening refrain from the lovely, meditative Fraction Anthem 171 in *The Hymnal 1982*:

Be known to us, Lord Jesus, in the breaking of the bread.

Introduce it first on your own, then invite participants to repeat it three more times with you.

Before moving on to Prayers, clean up crumbs, give people a chance to wash hands or get a drink of water and then reconvene.

Focus: Prayers

Overview of *The Book of Common Prayer*

We are what we pray. We become the words we speak. From ancient times, Christians have understood this: *lex orandi, lex credendi*: prayer establishes belief. In his book titled *Praying Shapes Believing*, Leonel Mitchell states that the Church "is first and foremost a worshiping community...the gathering together of the people of God for corporate worship, which is the heart and soul of the Church's life" (5).

Begin this part of the session by reminding your participants of Paul's words which they were given at the first session to carry with them: nothing—in heaven or on earth—nothing can separate them from the love of God in Jesus Christ. As they continue to carry and pray with those words, they will not only carve them into the soft tissue of their brains but will also mark their souls.

This ancient understanding of how our prayers shape our belief is confirmed by recent studies on language acquisition. The words we hear, read and speak literally do pattern our brains. Prayers, psalms, scripture passages that we learn become physically part of us; here again is the reminder that we inwardly digest these words. So, too, by the way, do repeated advertising slogans seek to gain entry, which is why we need to be as alert to what feeds our minds as to what feeds our bodies. We are what we eat, as the saying goes, but we are also the words we encounter.

This being so, the Episcopal Church is indeed fortunate to have *The Book of Common Prayer* as our identifying document. As Jeffrey Lee reminds us, "The prayer book does not offer precise doctrinal formulations that must be adhered to; rather, it provides the forms that outline our practice of the Christian faith, shaped principally by worship" (7). Through ongoing repetition of our common prayers, we shape our faith in God.

Pass out index cards again, and this time give participants 3 minutes to write down—on one side only—phrases they know from ads, words that Madison Avenue has engraved on their brains. You might begin by naming one or two that you recall. From my long-ago childhood, for example, I still remember "You can always tell a Halo girl. You can tell by the shine of her hair"; "Wonder Bread builds strong bodies eight ways"; and "Ajax! Boom! Boom! The foaming cleanser!" List below a few that you remember:

....

....

....

....

....

Stop them after 3 minutes and ask each participant to share one advertising slogan. Then ask them to turn the note card over and spend 3 minutes writing down phrases from prayers or scripture that they remember and treasure, holy words that are engraved in their minds and on their hearts. Share with them one or two of yours. Use the space below to note several prayers or passages that have been most important to you:

....

....

....

....

....

Again stop after 3 minutes and ask each participant to share one remembered prayer or passage.

Then ask participants to turn to page 810 in the prayer book to look at the list of all the Prayers and Thanksgivings collected there. Suggest that they look especially at pages 832-33, prayers 57-62, as they prepare to reaffirm their Baptismal Covenant. These prayers ask for guidance, confidence and protection; the last two are prayers of self-dedication.

If you have time, allow participants to browse through these pages. If some are already familiar with these prayers, ask for their experience using them. If you are pressed for time, simply encourage participants to become increasingly familiar with *The Book of Common Prayer* as part of their ongoing preparation.

(This is why it is so important for a parish to give participants a prayer book early in the program. Episcopalians are, remember, people of the book: *The Book of Common Prayer* is our identifying document. By using their own copy during this program, participants will build a relationship with it, which will make it a companion over the years, rather than a "graduation present" put away on a shelf.)

Before closing this session, remind the participants that prayers can come not only through words but from the silence of our hearts. Quote Thomas Cranmer's opening prayer at the Eucharist:

> *Almighty God, to you all hearts are open, all desires known, and from you no secrets are hid: Cleanse the thoughts of our hearts by the inspiration of your Holy Spirit, that we may perfectly love you, and worthily magnify your holy Name; through Christ our Lord. Amen.*

A simple naming of our desires, concerns and thanksgivings can be prayers of the heart. So can silence. William Shannon, for examples, talks of wanting to write a book on prayer "with a title page that would be followed by a hundred or more blank pages, with just the invitation at the beginning: 'Go through these pages slowly and silently'" (2).

Closing

Close this session with the prayer "For those about to be Baptized or to renew their Baptismal Covenant" on page 819 of the prayer book:

> *O God, you prepared your disciples for the coming of your Spirit through the teaching of your Son Jesus Christ: Make the hearts and minds of your servants ready to receive the blessing of the Holy Spirit, that they may be filled with his presence; through Jesus Christ our Lord. Amen.*

Then stand and sing your chosen hymn or recite the chosen canticle.

Ask participants to retrieve their chosen stones and step back into the circle.

Conclude with the exchange of the peace:

> *Leader:* The peace of the Lord be always with you.
> *Participants:* And also with you.

Blow out the candle.

After the Session

Looking Back, Looking Forward

Once all the participants have left, allow yourself a brief moment of reflection.

Where did you particularly feel God's grace among you during this session?

....
....
....
....
....

What do you wish had happened that didn't—or what did happen that you wish hadn't?

....
....
....
....
....

Offer it all to God, both the gracious and the grueling.

Be open to feel God's gratitude for your time and for your caring.

Go in peace, knowing that you have served God well.

Resist, Repent and Return

PLAN THE SESSION

Celebrant: *"Will you persevere in resisting evil, and, whenever you fall into sin, repent and return to the Lord?"*

People: *"I will, with God's help."*

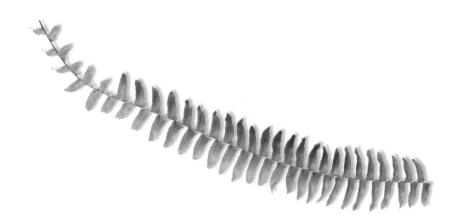

To Bring

- a candle and matches
- the communal psalm (if you've written it into this book, see p. 35)
- index cards
- small squares of thin paper that will fold and burn easily
- newsprint or large piece of paper or poster board
- a container in which to burn the pieces of paper, such as a cast iron pan or small grill (ensure proper ventilation; do outdoors, if necessary)
- pens and pencils
- extra Bibles
- prayer books (encourage participants to bring their own)
- leftover stones
- a watch or clock

Matters of Time

Single session: If you have a single session to cover this chapter, use one of the short Daily Devotions beginning on page 137 in *The Book of Common Prayer*. Try not to feel rushed. Don't give up the period of silence following the communal psalm.

Two sessions: If you have two sessions available, spend the first on evil, the second on repentance and return.

The Session(s) at a Glance

Gather

- light the candle
- set the stones
- read together the communal psalm
- maintain short silence
- share the appropriate service from *The Book of Common Prayer*

Activities

- focus on journal activities
  — reflections on Luke
  — reflections on sermon notes
- focus on "evil"
  — discussion of evil
  — writing prayers
- focus on "repentance and return"
  — reflections on the Prodigal Son
  — Litany of Penance
  — service of Reconciliation
- focus on the next session
  — prayer cards
  — preparation for next session

Closing

- sing chosen hymn or recite chosen canticle
- retrieve stones
- remind group members to use their journals between sessions
- exchange peace
- blow out candle

Leader's Reflection

This session names the reality of evil, the frailty of our human nature and the grace of God. The earliest, apostolic witness involved a call to repentance. These first witnesses defined Christ's saving action and called people to turn from sin to salvation, from death to life.

If you will be doing two sessions with this chapter, don't let participants leave feeling overwhelmed by the reality of evil. Close out the first session by repeating Paul's comforting words from Romans. Remind them that nothing, no evil in all the world, can separate them from the love and protection of God.

Think about your own perception of evil. What are some situations or actions or events in the world that you would label as evil? And where, in the aftermath, can you see God's tender presence?

....

....

....

....

When in your own life have you confronted evil? How did you know? How did you respond? What would you do differently? Where was God?

....

....

....

....

The Baptismal Covenant uses the phrase "fall into sin." What does it actually feel like when you know you have done wrong? What other verbs might you use besides "fall"?

....

....

....

....

....

What public acts of repentance have you heard about from history or literature as well as current times that might make effective examples for your participants?

....

....

....

....

Think about your own experience with repentance, with deep regret and sorrow for the sin. Can you think of a situation you would be willing to share with the group?

....

....

....

....

Returning, turning away from the wrong direction and back towards God, is a joyful homecoming. Write down a few actual "homecomings" (family gatherings, episodes of reconciliation and return, etc.) when you knew that God had "put away" your sin and that you had come home to God.

....

....

....

Your participants' journals take them through the Litany of Penitence from the Ash Wednesday service, beginning on page 267 in the prayer book. You will lead them through it again during the session. You need to review it yourself ahead of time, to allow reflective time with those petitions, to identify your own particular temptations.

Just as you and all the participants are already baptized, already full members of the household of faith, so too are all sinners who fall short of the mark. Sit awhile with your own tendencies and temptations, and with God's saving action in your life. Be able to name one of those sins to which you are prone.

Be Tender to Yourself

Continue to ask the parish's prayers for yourself as well as for the participants in the program, and allow yourself to feel God's gratitude for the work you do. Remember that you are a child of God, infinitely loved and precious. No matter how this session goes, God is at work among you , and all will be well.

What are your biggest fears or biggest hopes for this session on evil and repentance? Write them below, and offer them to God.

....

....

....

....

....

Before the Session

Before the participants arrive set up the table and chairs as in earlier sessions with a candle, a Bible and *The Book of Common Prayer* on the table. This time also add the container in which you will "burn" the collective sins of the group. Put prayer books beside each chair (unless your generous parish has given each participant his or her own prayer book already, and you know they will be bringing them).

THE SESSION

Gather

Once everyone has arrived, gather in a circle around the table. Tell the participants that once you have lit the candle, they should step forward, set their stone and as they say their names, they should follow up with a statement from the Litany of Penitence (from their journals). Give them time to look at what they wrote while you offer an example, such as "John Smith. Guilty of uncharitable thoughts toward others" or "Mary Smith. I've been negligent in prayer and worship" or "Mel Smith. I'm pretty blind to human need and suffering." Allow participants the option of praying these sentences aloud or to themselves. Once everyone seems ready and attentive again, place your stone near the candle and name both yourself and one of your categories of sin.

Once everyone has helped "build the altar" this week, ask them to get out their copy of the communal psalm, find a comfortable sitting position, breathe deeply and get ready during the silence to rest in God's loving presence, knowing that despite our sins we are beloved children of God. Explain how you will pray their psalm this time, whether in unison or responsively, then begin.

> *Leader:* The Lord be with you.
> *Participants:* And also with you.
> *Leader:* Let us pray:

Pray the psalm. Then time the silence. (Allow at least two minutes; consider extending the time if it won't make you feel too rushed. Being able to sit in shared silence for between ten and twenty minutes by the final session would be ideal.)

End the silence by praying the Lord's Prayer together. Then lead the group in whatever service you have selected ahead of time from *The Book of Common Prayer*.

Focus: Journal Activities

Luke

Unless you had a marathon session during which you read all of Luke aloud, your participants have begun reading it on their own. Before going into the focus on sin and repentance, take time to ask for any questions about what they read. After responding to any questions, simply go around the circle and ask each participant to read one quotation they recorded from Luke, even if half the people ahead of them recorded the same one. (It's always good to hear familiar stories.)

Sermon Notes

Then ask if anyone has comments, quotes or questions they want to share in connection with a recent sermon. If so, take the time to respond, encouraging others to join in. Afterwards move ahead to the core of the session.

Focus: Resisting Evil

Discussion

Begin by having participants turn to page 304 in the prayer book; read the question for this session, asking them to respond appropriately:

> *Leader:* Will you persevere in resisting evil, and, whenever you fall into sin, repent and return to the Lord?
>
> *Participants:* I will, with God's help.

The primary clause—hence the primary emphasis—of this session's question deals with evil: "Will you persevere in resisting evil..." Then, recognizing human frailty, "*whenever* you fall into sin," the question goes on to ask if you will "repent and return to the Lord." But the question of evil comes first. The Rev. Lewis Sligh says that resisting evil is a particularly difficult promise because our current concept of evil is so undefined. "Evil," he says, "comes in all different shades, from genocide to cheating on income tax."

We live in an age that has a hard time using the term "evil" at all. We'd rather find some other excuse, some other, less threatening name, yet Wright reminds us that "Evil is real and powerful. It is not only 'out there,' in other people, but it is present and active in each of us" (71). Modern psychology tells us that the things that happen to us predispose us to certain behaviors, but they do not force us to do them.

Years ago, Ellen Goodman wrote an editorial about what she called the "last sin in America"—being overweight. I remember her saying that Americans would excuse a murderer because of some childhood trauma while condemning a friend for putting on a few pounds. Acknowledging responsibility (*mea* culpa—not "mom's fault" or "the devil made me do it") is a necessary part in resisting evil.

 "Understanding why one does wrong is *not* the same as excusing it. Every one of us belongs to God and is responsible for our own actions," insists the Rev. Ellen Shaver. Real healing (real repentance and return) happens only when we name our own capacity for evil and we take personal responsibility for our lives. Sligh names the shootings at Columbine High School as a "personification of the evil that lives in our society. The boys weren't evil, but they fell into sin and did a very evil thing. There's a problem when people excuse the action because they don't want to condemn the actor. We need to hold ourselves and one another accountable."

In other words, evil is real, it is around us and we are called to resist it. When we don't, when we fall into sin and commit evil, we are accountable for those choices. God does not abandon us; but through our choices we sometimes abandon God.

Another problem in talking about "evil" is that too often we have in our heads the image of a "good" Christian who is utterly naive and we think that's how we all should be. We misrepresent the distinction between "good" and "evil," thinking that being good means being absurdly innocent. We need to remember, however, that Jesus also admonishes us to be "wise as serpents" in order to recognize and resist evil. I remember the Rev. Tom Hansen years ago reiterating, "Jesus died to take away your sins, not your mind!"

After talking briefly about evil, go around the circle asking each participant, "How did you *resist* evil in the past week?"

Depending on the nature of your group, you could then ask them about the hardest battle they fought with evil—and won. Try to generate some ideas about *how* people go about resisting evil. You might tell them about the Church of the Holy Nativity in Baltimore, which meets in a converted auto parts store across the street from where drug dealers operate. Most of us don't face the kind of visible and violent evil that those parishioners face daily. Describe how "Mother Vicki" has her confirmands memorize passages from scripture, prayers and hymns as armor against evil.

What armor or anchors do participants in your program use to resist evil and fight temptation? This next activity asks them to consider that question.

Prayers Against Temptation

Ask the group members to turn to page 832 in the prayer book and look at prayers 52-62. Then ask them to work in pairs (or threes) to compose a very brief prayer that one could repeat in the face of temptation. Pass out index cards to each pair and let them work for about 5 minutes. Then ask participants to read their prayers aloud. Offer them time to copy one or more of the prayers into their journals.

Focus: Repent and Return

Prodigal Son

The Baptismal Covenant asks, "Will you persevere in resisting evil," knowing that we can't. So it includes, "whenever you fall into sin, repent and return to the Lord." This is good news for us because it takes human beings seriously. We are going to fail and fall, over and over again, but provision is made.

The history of our relationship with God involves rules which human beings continue to break. In Eden, there was one rule; after the flood, Noah was given three; at Sinai, Moses received ten commandments; the traditional counting of rules in the whole of the Torah numbers 613: 248 telling us what to do, 365 telling us what *not* to do. "We break them all," says the Rev. Ellen Shaver. "We break them all."

At the end of Luke's gospel, Jesus commissions his disciples to ensure that in his name "repentance for the forgiveness of sins be preached to all nations, beginning from Jerusalem. You are witnesses of this." Karl Barth says that the church needs, loudly and often, to proclaim "the free grace of God and the hope which this carries with it" (*Church Dogmatics* 65). Shaver echoes Barth: "We, too, have been forgiven much by God. We have been saved by grace—the unmerited, unearned, undeserved love of God." We need to confront our sins, those places where our perseverance in resisting evil wavered. We need to confess those sins and choose to live an intentional life in Christ.

Once they reassemble after writing and sharing their prayers of protection, read the Parable of the Prodigal Son aloud in a slow, meditative fashion (beginning at Luke 15:11). Remind them that this is from the gospel account that they are reading at home. If time allows, you could ask a participant to read the parable aloud again (or do so yourself), giving people a chance to savor, to inwardly digest, the message. Give participants index cards before the final reading and ask them to write down words, phrases or images that strike them. Ask them to consider where this story touches places in their own lives.

After the final reading, allow a moment of silence, then give each person a chance to respond.

Litany of Penitence

At this point, hand out the thin paper and explain that you would like them to write down those sins that rose in their memories as they went through the Litany of Penitence in their journals. Give them a chance to turn chairs around or otherwise seek privacy while they do this. Tell them to fold the paper up when they are done in preparation for burning it.

Once all participants have written down their sins, ask them to turn to page 267 in the prayer book and lead them through the Litany of Penitence. End at the top of 269 with these words:

Bring us with all your saints to the joy of his resurrection.

Reconciliation

Next direct the participants to Form Two of Reconciliation on page 449. Show them how it is set up. Tell them that when you reach "Especially I confess..." on page 450 you will pause for silence instead of asking for "particular sins" to be named aloud, and when you get to the laying on of hands on 451, instead of doing that you will go directly to the Declaration of Forgiveness on page 452.

(If it is a viable option in your parish, encourage each participant to arrange for the Sacrament of Reconciliation sometime prior to reaffirming their baptismal vows. Your parish could make available the book *Reconciliation*, written by Episcopal monastic Martin Smith, SSJE.)

Now is the time to kindle a small fire and burn the sins which have just been forgiven. Invite participants to come forward one at a time and set their sins in the container, lighting a match and setting fire to their folded paper. Lewis Sligh suggests the option of putting the folded papers into envelopes, sealing them and saving them to burn in the New Fire kindled for the Easter Vigil. This would be meaningful only if you are conducting this program during Lent, and if your parish already observes the full Easter Vigil liturgy.

In any event, whenever you burn these, remind the participant of such theological images as the burning bush and the pillar of fire. Remind them, too, that not only does fire consume—it also transforms. Fire takes dark matter and transfigures it. If you routinely share a snack or a meal at these gatherings, this would be an appropriate time to share food as a way of sharing in the feast thrown for the Prodigal Son, since the participants, too, are celebrating forgiveness for their sins.

Once the sins are burned (or put away in envelopes to be burned at the Easter Vigil), tell them that repentance, from the Greek *metanoia*, means a literal change of direction, not just a change of heart. On the newsprint, or on a black (or white) board, draw an imaginary road map for someone's life, including ups and downs but largely going in one direction. Stop, then show how true repentance would literally change the direction of the journey. (You could use as a model the Prodigal Son's life.)

Another way to think about repentance is that it draws us from error into truth. The word "error" comes from the Latin *errare*, meaning to wander. In other words, when we sin or err or stray ("like lost sheep"), we get off the right path. The Hebrew word for sin, *het*, means missing the mark.

These are all words that describe direction. When we sin, we miss the mark and wander off in the wrong direction until repentance turns us toward the right goal: a life in Christ, through whom God has "delivered us from evil, and...brought us out of error into truth, out of sin into righteousness, out of death into life." Help participants find the place in their journals where they can draw their own road maps.

Focus: The Next Session

Prayer Cards

Ask participants to get out their prayer card with a participant's name, to turn it over and write, "You have been in my prayers," then to sign their names and pass the card to the person on their right. (If some end up with their own names, tell them to be especially conscious of praying for themselves this week; next week they will pass the card on. We aren't always good about looking after ourselves, including praying for ourselves. Being asked to pray for oneself with special intentionality is not a bad thing.)

Optional: Preparations

If you have instrumental musicians among your participants, consider asking them to bring instruments as background accompaniment to the communal psalm next week. This could include flute, guitar, cello, trumpet, drums, harmonica—invite creativity.

Closing

Close this session as you have the others with the prayer "For those about to be Baptized or to renew their Baptismal Covenant" on page 819 of the prayer book:

> O God, you prepared your disciples for the coming of your Spirit through the teaching of your Son Jesus Christ: Make the hearts and minds of your servants ready to receive the blessing of the Holy Spirit, that they may be filled with his presence; through Jesus Christ our Lord. Amen.

Then stand and sing your chosen hymn or recite the chosen canticle.

Have participants retrieve their chosen stones and step back into the circle.

Conclude with the exchange of the peace

Leader: The peace of the Lord be always with you.
Participants: And also with you.

Blow out the candle.

After the Session

Looking Back, Looking Forward

Once all the participants have left, allow yourself a brief moment of reflection.

Where did you particularly feel God's grace among you during this session?

....
....
....
....
....

What do you wish had happened that didn't—or what did happen that you wish hadn't?

....
....
....
....
....

Offer it all to God, both the gracious and the grueling.

Be open to feel God's gratitude for your time and for your caring.

Go in peace, knowing that you have served God well.

By Word and Example

PLAN THE SESSION

Celebrant: *"Will you proclaim by word and example the Good News of God in Christ?"*

People: *"I will, with God's help."*

To Bring

- a candle and matches
- big kitchen matches
- a flashlight if needed to read by
- the communal psalm composed at the first session
- the "secular creed" from earlier session
- index cards
- pens and pencils
- extra Bibles
- prayer books (unless they will bring their own)
- the leftover stones
- a watch (if no clock is visible)
- *Lesser Feasts and Fasts* (if available) or any book of saints
- a recent copy of People magazine
- icons of saints (or reproductions of art based on scripture)

Optional:
- music: either live music, as in members of the choir or other musicians, or a recording of Gregorian chant or other sacred music
- flowers

Matters of Time

Single session: If you have only a single session to cover this chapter, use as your service the appropriate short Daily Devotions beginning on page 137 in *The Book of Common Prayer*, and continue to assign more of Luke to be read at home, again reminding the participants that reading scripture is always a communal act, even when done in solitude. *Do not give up the brief period of silence. Do not feel rushed.*

Two sessions: If you have two sessions for this chapter, spend the first on "word" and the second on "example." Consider using one of the complete Morning, Noonday or Evening Prayer services in *The Book of Common Prayer*.

Longer/retreat session: The material in this chapter could also be done in a day-long (or overnight) retreat, with built-in time for contemplative prayer, and several shared meals. In such a setting, it would be appropriate to gather throughout the day for Morning, Noonday and Evening Prayer services. If you have time, opportunity and willing participants, you could arrange a movie session, consider a trip to an art museum or an evening of sacred music.

The Session(s) at a Glance

Gather

- light the candle
- set the stones
- read together the communal psalm
- maintain short silence
- share the appropriate service from *The Book of Common Prayer*

Activities

- focus on proclaiming the word
  — light witness matches
  — examine the witness of saints and heroes
  — read "secular creed" and contrast with the Good News of God in Christ
  — read "commissioning" passages from scripture
- focus on journal activities
  — reflections on Luke
  — reflections on sermon notes
- focus on word and example
  — sermon of our selves
  — service
  — beauty of holiness
- focus on next week's session
  — praying for one another
  — preparations

Closing

- sing chosen hymn or recite chosen canticle
- retrieve stones
- remind group members to use their journals between sessions
- exchange peace
- blow out candle

Leader's Reflection

This session is about witnessing. As leader of this program, you are already a witness to God's Word; already you exemplify what you will be teaching the participants.

Think about people over the years whose witness was important to you, people who, by word and example, witnessed to the Good News of God in Christ. Name them; as you write, offer a prayer of gratitude for their witness:

....
....
....
....
....

Besides leading this program, how else in the past year have you been a witness to Christ?

....
....
....
....
....

Which among those episodes of witnessing would you be most comfortable sharing with the group?

....
....
....
....
....

Remember that those participating in this program are also witnesses to the Good News of God in Christ. As the Rev. Justin Lindstrom says, "In the Episcopal Church, our confirmation is our altar call." Renewing our Baptismal Covenant is a mature and public witness to our covenant relationship with God.

Be Tender to Yourself

Continue to ask the congregation's prayers for yourself as well as for the participants in your program, and allow yourself to feel God's gratitude for this work you do. Remember that you are a child of God, infinitely loved and precious. No matter how each session goes, God is at work among you all, and all will be well.

What are your biggest fears or biggest hopes for this session? Write them below, and offer them to God.

....

....

....

....

....

Before the Session

Before the participants arrive put the usual table in the middle of the room, and on it place a candle, a Bible, *The Book of Common Prayer*, icons of saints or reproductions of sacred art (post card reproductions are fine) and perhaps beautifully arranged flowers.

Place a prayer book on or beside each chair if participants still don't have their own.

A note on reading the communal psalm: you might consider having each participant read his or her own verse, or try alternating male and female voices, or going in order around the circle, verse by verse, or even having musical background accompaniment.

THE SESSION

Gather

If possible, have either live or recorded music in progress as people arrive. Once everyone has arrived, gather in a circle around the table. Remind them that this session deals with proclaiming God's good news to the world by word and example. Point out the music, art, arranged flowers, whatever examples of aesthetic witness you have been able to gather. Note that there are many ways to "speak" the word of God, and words are only one of those ways.

Ask the participants to think about ways they have somehow "proclaimed the Good News of God in Christ" during the past week. What is one act or endeavor that embodied faithful living or that offered praise to God? As they set their stones, they should say their names, and name one act of proclamation at home, or at work, or at school, or among friends. After you light the candle, place your own stone nearby on the table, articulate your name, tell one example of how you have "proclaimed the Good News" this week, then step back.

Once the participants have all arranged their stones and named themselves and their witness, ask them to sit down and find their copy of the communal psalm. Read it together either in unison, or by having each participant read his or her own verse, or by going around the circle, or by alternating male and female voices. This would also be an excellent week to make use of any instrumental musicians to accompany the recitations since music is one kind of "example" by which people proclaim the Good News of God in Christ. Continue to experiment with ways of sharing the communal psalm. This is, after all, the "joyful noise" which this particular group composed for the Lord; make it as joyful as possible.

Remind them that there will be a brief period of silence (2-5 minutes or more) after the psalm. Ask them to find a comfortable position in their chairs, to breathe deeply, and, during the silence, to focus on a line from the psalm, on the name of Jesus or simply on their own rhythmic breathing as they rest in God's presence.

Remaining seated, lead the participants in reciting their psalm. Then time the silence. (Don't quit too soon; be sure to allow at least 2 full minutes.)

End the silence by praying the Lord's Prayer together. Then lead the group in whatever service you routinely use.

Focus: Proclaim by Word

Lighting Matches

"Jesus Christ is the Word of God spoken to all. As I, too, am one of the all, and as I, too, believing and hoping in his promise, may see myself as one who is addressed by his Word, I am empowered, commissioned, and liberated with heart and hand and voice to bear witness to him as this Word of the love of God" (Barth, *Final* 4).

Darken the room as much as possible. Ask participants to stand fairly close together. Pass out a big kitchen match to each person. Recite 1 Peter 2:9: "You are a chosen race, a royal priesthood, a holy nation, God's own people, in order that you may proclaim the mighty acts of him who called you out of darkness into his marvelous light." (Use a flashlight to read that by if the candle isn't bright enough.)

Tell them that you will pass the matchbox so that one at a time participants can light their matches. While the match burns down, each participant in turn says everything that comes to mind about God. You begin. Strike your match, and while it burns, simply say everything that comes to mind about God. (If the match doesn't go out on its own, blow it out before it burns your fingers.) Then pass the box.

Once everyone is done, turn lights back on. Explain that the Australian prayer book, in its notes on the confirmation service, says that "Christians should be willing to confess their faith publicly (Romans 10:9-13)." This doesn't necessarily mean lighting matches on street corners, but it does imply responsibility in terms of owning, claiming and witnessing to one's faith by word and example. Bishop Chilton Knudsen describes the "amazing witness" of a fifteen-year-old confirmand who composed a letter to her estranged father explaining why she felt called to confirmation in the Episcopal Church: "I want to belong to Jesus Christ in this way," she wrote. "I'm sorry you won't be there."

John's gospel begins with "In the beginning was the Word." The Greek word for "word," *logos*, doesn't just refer to the spoken word but encompasses the connecting part of reality, "the thread on which the necklace of creation is strung," as Lewis Sligh says, "planets and universes strung on the Word, this thread."

Then the prologue of John switches images from Word to Light: the Word becomes so real it becomes luminous. This is Transfiguration language, yet interestingly the gospel of John has no Transfiguration until the actual crucifixion. For John, the crucifixion is where people see Jesus' glory-except instead of being flanked by Moses and Elijah, now Jesus is flanked by two criminals.

By showing Jesus transfigured even on the cross, John tells us that even in the midst of terrible suffering we can still proclaim by word and example. Nothing exempts us from this baptismal promise.

Saints and Heroes

One way to look at such witness is to examine the lives of the saints, many of whom faced terrible situations, often with surprising joy. Saints are the word of Christ spoken in the world. If you have a copy of *Lesser Feasts and Fasts*, pass it around to let participants see the array of saints' days in our Episcopal calendar, or read about a few of your favorites. Point out the Calendar beginning on page 19 in the prayer book and ask them if their birthday falls on a saint's day. If you have icons or religious paintings depicting saints, tell a little about them. Remind participants that saints' stories are our stories, too, since they form part of our extended family.

Several years ago the prompt to which students responded on the SAT II: Writing Test dealt with the loss of stature in contemporary "heroes." Many students agreed that the contemporary world has no real heroes left. Yet others named Mother Teresa and Martin Luther King, Jr. as well as members of their family or community as people who still deserved the designation "hero."

Pass out index cards and ask each participant to write down (privately) the name of a "hero" they admire. The person could be living or dead, someone they've met, someone they've read about or someone they've seen only on television or in the movies.

Collect and shuffle the cards, then pass them out randomly. If some get their cards own back, they can keep them. Ask each participant to explain why the named person on the card they are holding could be considered a hero. If it is a name they do not know at all, they can ask help from the group. Perhaps only the person who wrote that card will be able to describe that "hero." This procedure will elicit more involvement than simply having each participant name his or her "hero."

Once everyone has described the "hero" on his or her card, see if there are any common threads, any characteristics of heroes. What "word" or "example" do they offer the world? Which ones might be called "saints"? Affirm that we are *all* called to be saints.

Secular Creeds and Heroes

Now get out the combined secular creeds they composed earlier and read them aloud. (If you have had time to type them up as a single long creed, pass it out to them.) Ask who the contemporary secular heroes are according to *that* particular set of "beliefs." Allow time for them to discuss current American "heroes." Do any appear on the original list of "saints and heroes"?

After some discussion, remind them of the need to hold onto the counter-cultural image of life which the Baptismal Covenant offers. To be serious about confirmation means to take the gospel message seriously—and over and over again, that message involves witness.

Note: Acknowledge that in our pluralistic society there is tension between *active* and *overactive* evangelism. As Lewis Sligh points out, it's easier to ask someone, "Have you accepted Jesus?" than to *live* as an example of Christ's love in the world. "[As an] example...we live out the Word that's living in us." Sligh recalls a rabbi's response to the Baptist prayers for the conversion of the Jews during their High Holy Days: "We could use a little less love and a little more respect."

Commissioning

The concluding action of Jesus Christ is to commission his disciples. In Mark's "long ending," the very disciples who had just been chastised for hardness of heart and lack of faith for failing to believe the resurrection are now sent as witnesses of it. In John's gospel, Jesus tells his close friends, "As the Father has sent me, so do I send you."

What this means, as Raymond Brown points out, is that "now must the disciples in their mission manifest the presence of Jesus to the point that whoever sees the disciples sees Jesus who sent them. That is an enormous challenge!" (75) And it is our challenge, too. We are to so live the Word that we become luminous enough for others to see Christ in us.

Matthew, too, records the commissioning of the disciples to go quickly and share their joy with others. And in Acts, Jesus says, "Ye shall be my witnesses both in Jerusalem, and in all Judea and Samaria, and unto the uttermost parts of the earth." Here we are, across an ocean, at one of the uttermost parts of the earth, and we are to proclaim by word and example the Good News of God in Christ. We are, as latter day disciples, sent into the world in witness.

Ask participants to discuss:
• How does baptism serve as the "commissioning" of disciples?
• How can we keep our commission in mind as we prepare for confirmation?

Focus: Journal Activities

Luke

As witnesses, we need to know the Good News which we are to proclaim, so this would be a good time to review what participants have to say about their reading in Luke since the last session. Respond to questions, encourage commentary and ask each participant to share at least one quotation from their Notes and Quotes from Luke.

Sermon Notes

Then spend time dealing with reactions to sermons. This week, emphasize that preaching is a form of witness. Protestant theologian Karl Barth actually called preaching a sacrament if the preacher has indeed listened to the Holy Spirit during the planning and writing of the sermon.

Episcopalians might question elevating the sermon to the status of sacrament, but it's good to remember the high regard in which preaching the Word is held—it shouldn't be something one "endures" but something that opens avenues to understanding. Encourage the participants to share ways they have found to keep their hearts open and listening.

Note: If you plan to take at least two sessions for this chapter, this would be an appropriate place to close this session.

Focus: Proclaiming by Word and Example

Sermon of Our Selves

"God's power enables us to make commitments and be accountable, to will and to work for God's good pleasure" (Ellen Shaver). God gives us the grace, but we need to claim it. We need to be accountable to the gospel we are to proclaim. This is why participants are reading all of Luke. This is why regular church attendance is assumed among those seeking to renew their Baptismal Covenants. This is why Vicki Sirota works so hard to instill the words of scripture in her confirmands' minds. We need to know the story before we can proclaim it.

Back in 1941, Dorothy Sayers bemoaned "the brutal fact is that in this Christian country not one person in a hundred has the faintest notion what the Church teaches about God or man or society or the person of Jesus Christ" (31). Your participants are no longer among that ignorant majority; but the more they know, the greater their responsibility to live out that knowledge.

The stories we read and internalize determine in some measure who we are. Just as praying shapes believing, so do other words shape us. "There is no such thing as resistance to influence," Ellen Charry tells us; "there is at most a choice among influences" (By 22).

Jon Krakauer's account of Christopher McCandless's journey *Into the Wild* shows the danger of taking the wrong story to heart. McCandless read Thoreau, London and Tolstoy and he believed them. He did not take time to find out that they were fallible men who went home for Sunday dinner, or who drank too much, or who burdened a wife with thirteen children while preaching celibacy. He took their words as gospel without examining their lives, and it cost him *his* life. Those stories had given him an identity as a fiercely independent, highly moral loner. He died alone in the wilderness, of starvation compounded by illness.

And yet one is tempted to say that Chris's choices were still better than flashy advertisements as something to believe in. Barbara Brown Taylor says that slick ads "appeal to the same part of us that holy images do, and in many ways the ongoing struggle of faith is the struggle to choose between those [images] that have power to save us and those that do not" (42). Our material culture tells us stories every day, stories that try to make us feel like fat, poorly dressed, inept, unclean, uncool losers.

Jesus tells us differently. Our Christian story calls us beloved children of God. "Up to this very day the Spirit calls into being the existence of every single Christian as a believing, loving, hoping witness to the Word of God" (Barth, *Evangelical* 55). This is the message we need to share.

Pass out index cards and ask your participants, first, to write down this question, and, second, to answer it: "If the gospel is my story, and if my life is meant to be a living sermon, what did I just preach today?" Give them about 3 minutes to respond, then ask for answers. This activity should help them begin to see beyond proclaiming with just words and recognize as well how they proclaim with their actions.

Service

Bishop Knudsen says, "What you say with your mouth is one thing. How you spend time, money and relational resources is another." We need to live the Word, not just speak it. Our lives are witnesses to Christ; we need to be careful what our lives say. Mother Teresa once said that a word of kindness can be the Incarnation of Christ, but she always supported her kind words with hard labor in the field of her Lord.

If you are incorporating a service component into this program, this would be an appropriate time to discuss how it is going, or to introduce what it will be. Help participants be aware, first of all, of the ways in which their daily lives *already* call them to service.

Ask participants to name what elements of service exist in their daily work and in their daily household situations. Emphasize possibilities of service that do not simply bring us into contact with our families and peers, but with the stranger, the demanding, the difficult. Help participants identify these possibilities, and discuss together ways we can serve effectively in our daily lives. For some participants, faithful attention to these daily possibilities for service will be all their schedules can accommodate. Affirm the contributions of these participants, too.

Ideally, participants in this program will commit to outside service through a local organization. When my nephew was in preparation for confirmation, for example, he went regularly to visit a patient at an inner-city nursing home in Boston. One of my tenth grade students organized her confirmation group to raise money for Brunswick's homeless shelter. In the case of my student, a chance encounter with a homeless teenager in New York City had sent her back to Maine determined to make a difference. She did.

Help participants decide together how they can make a difference through active striving.

Beauty of Holiness

Another kind of service to God and to the Church—and this cycles back to the beginning of the session—is "to create the beauty of holiness" through such ministries as music, art, writing, flower arranging, altar guild work: everything that goes into the aesthetic elements of worship (Micks 92). To wind down the session, you could play sacred music, read some of George Herbert's or John Donne's religious poetry, pass around icons or reproductions of religious art. If you have time available, you could even watch one of the suggested films or play a piece of sacred music all the way through, or you could arrange a field trip to a museum or a concert.

Tell the participants to look attentively at the world around them during the time between sessions, to notice the different ways that people are witnessing to the gospel message, living lives that show the living Word. When I was growing up, the words

"Let your light so shine..." always meant to reach for the wallet. Ask participants to find a variety of ways to let their light shine, to become so luminous that the light of Christ shines through them.

Focus: Next Week's Session

Prayer Cards

Ask participants to get out their prayer card with a participant's name, to turn it over and write, "You have been in my prayers," then to sign their names and pass the card to the person on their right. (If some end up with their own names, tell them to be especially conscious of praying for themselves this week; next week they will pass the card on. We aren't always good about looking after ourselves, including praying for ourselves. Being asked to pray for oneself with special intentionality is not a bad thing.)

Preparations

Tell participants that next week they will experience footwashing. Suggest that they wear easily-removable footwear.

Closing

Close this session as you have the others with the prayer "For those about to be Baptized or to renew their Baptismal Covenant" on page 819 of the prayer book:

O God, you prepared your disciples for the coming of your Spirit through the teaching of your Son Jesus Christ: Make the hearts and minds of your servants ready to receive the blessing of the Holy Spirit, that they may be filled with his presence; through Jesus Christ our Lord. Amen.

Then stand and sing your chosen hymn or recite the chosen canticle.

Have participants retrieve their chosen stones and step back into the circle.

Conclude with the exchange of the peace:

Leader: The peace of the Lord be always with you.
Participants: And also with you.

Blow out the candle.

After the Session

Looking Back, Looking Forward

Once all the participants have left, allow yourself a brief moment of reflection.

Where did you particularly feel God's grace among you during this session?

....
....
....
....
....

What do you wish had happened that didn't—or what did happen that you wish hadn't?

....
....
....
....
....

Offer it all to God, both the gracious and the grueling.

Be open to feel God's gratitude for your time and for your caring.

Go in peace, knowing that you have served God well.

Seek and Serve

PLAN THE SESSION

Celebrant: *"Will you seek and serve Christ in all persons, loving your neighbor as yourself?"*

People: *"I will, with God's help."*

To Bring

- a candle and matches
- the communal psalm
- a basin or bowl for footwashing
- a large pitcher filled with warm water
- several towels (one towel per six participants)
- a tightly wound ball of yarn
- index cards
- pens/pencils
- extra Bibles
- prayer books
- the left-over stones

- a watch (if no clock is visible)
- a recording of sacred music to play during the footwashing (and the necessary equipment on which to play it), or a brief anthem or Taize meditation that you can teach participants to sing quietly during the footwashing

Matters of Time

Single session: If you have only a single session to cover this chapter, use as your service the appropriate short Daily Devotions beginning on page 137 in *The Book of Common Prayer*.

Two sessions: If you have two sessions for this chapter, spend the first week on the proposed activities up through The Great Litany; save the footwashing for the second session. Choose your service depending on time available. With two sessions, you can also consider inviting a parishioner who is involved in a regular prayer group to come and talk about prayer as service.

Longer/retreat session: The material in this chapter could also be done in a day-long (or overnight) retreat, with time for contemplative prayer, longer story-telling sessions, a film and several shared meals. In such a setting, it would be appropriate to gather throughout the day for Morning, Noonday and Evening Prayer services. If you have time for a film, either during a session or separately, you could show *Brother Sun, Sister Moon* about St. Francis.

The Session(s) at a Glance

Gather

- light the candle
- set the stones, naming servants
- read together the communal psalm
- maintain short silence
- share the appropriate service from *The Book of Common Prayer*

Activities

- focus on journal activities
  — reflections on Luke
  — reflections on sermon notes
- focus on seeking Christ in others
  — stories
  — yarn web
  — intercessory prayer
- focus on loving neighbors as ourselves
  — caring for self
  — Good Samaritan
  — footwashing

- focus on the next session
  — praying for one another

Closing

- sing chosen hymn or recite chosen canticle
- retrieve stones
- remind group members to use their journals between sessions
- exchange peace
- blow out candle

Leader's Reflection

"[T]he real business of the Christian life," says Roberta Bondi, is not lofty discussion of spiritual matters but "to love God with all our hearts, souls, strength, and mind, and our neighbors as ourselves" (20). This session is about the familiar Golden Rule: "Do unto others as you would have them do unto you." The danger is that its very familiarity keeps people from truly hearing what it says.

Spend some time before leading this session thinking about how you care for yourself and others. Be able to name those whom you serve, and those who serve you. As leader, you are a role model of the Christian life. This session reminds us we are to love and care for ourselves. What are ways you do this?

....

....

....

....

(If that space is blank, fill it with ways you would *like* to take care of yourself, and consider ways of actually doing so.)

What are ways in which you care for others? (Remember to include leading this program.)

....

....

....

....

....

....

....

As you look at your list, consider whether you consciously see Christ in those you serve.

Now list all those who have served and cared for you over the years, treating you as though you were Christ himself:

....

....

....

....

....

When have you felt most loved by your "neighbors"? by an intimate? by a stranger? by God?

....

....

....

....

....

Be Tender to Yourself

Continue to ask the congregation's prayers for yourself as well as for the participants in your program, and allow yourself to feel God's gratitude for this work you do. Remember that you are a child of God, infinitely loved and precious. No matter how each session goes, God is at work among you all, and all will be well. What are your biggest fears or biggest hopes for this session? Write them below, and offer them to God.

....

....

....

....

....

Before the Session

Before the participants arrive set up the table as usual with candle, Bible and prayer book. This time also place a basin or bowl, the pitcher filled with water, towels and the ball of tightly wound yarn. Put chairs in a circle, and (if participants still don't have their own) put prayer books out.

Decide how you want to structure the footwashing. Either you can model servant leadership by washing all their feet, or you can wash one person's feet and pass the task along so that they wash one another's feet. You can also either station the water and towels in one location and have people come there, or you (and others) can take the basin and towels around the circle while participants remain seated. (This is my preference since there is more of a sense of being served if one remains seated; if the participants also do some of the footwashing, they get to experience both being seated and being on the floor washing someone else's feet.)

If you have participants who might find the necessary bending or floor-sitting awkward or painful, consider being the sole footwasher—unless doing so would be painful for you. If for some reason footwashing is utterly impossible, see the suggestion for handwashing later in the session. (In other words, do some thinking about logistics **before the session**.)

If you want to have members of a prayer group address this session on seeking and serving Christ in others, be sure to invite them well ahead of time.

THE SESSION

Gather

Once everyone has arrived, gather in a circle around the table. Tell them that this time as they set their stones, they should not only name themselves, but also name someone who has "served" them, someone who has treated them tenderly, as though honoring the Christ within them. Give an example:

> "Paula Nomizu. My fourth grade teacher Mrs. Hernandez served me well."

> "Francis Doherty. My Aunt Mary treated me tenderly."

> "Jane Springer. A stranger on the subway was kind to me."

Light the candle. Speak your name and the name of someone who served you or treated you as though you were Christ. Step back and let the participants do the same.

Sit down, but before you share the communal psalm, tell them that you will be leading them in a guided meditation during the period of silence this time, one that will help them focus on caring for themselves and for others. Then recite together the communal psalm; continue to experiment with ways of reading it. If you tried instrumental background last time and it worked well, keep it up.

After the psalm, remind participants to find a comfortable position, to close their eyes, to breathe deeply, to feel themselves resting in God's presence. The following guided meditation is adapted from a retreat led by the Rev. Jack McCall in Portland, Maine in 1993. Once everyone is settled, repeat the following prayers slowly, pausing for at least three deep breaths after each recitation:

"May I be at peace. May I know the beauty of my own true nature. May my heart remain open. May I be healed."

Remember: pray it slowly. Pause for at least three slow, silent breaths before going on.

"May all of us gathered here be at peace. May we all know the beauty of our own true natures. May our hearts remain open. May we be healed."

Remember: pray it slowly. Pause for at least three breaths before going on.

"May those we love be at peace. May they know the beauty of their own true natures. May their hearts remain open. May they be healed."

Remember: pray it slowly. Pause for at least three breaths before going on.

"May all people in this (community , town, city) be at peace. May they know the beauty of their own true natures. May their hearts remain open. May they be healed."

Remember: pray it slowly. Pause for at least three breaths before going on.

"May all people throughout the world be at peace. May they know the beauty of their own true natures. May their hearts remain open. May they be healed."

Remember: pray it slowly. Pause for at least three breaths before going on to this last (first) prayer.

"May I be at peace. May I know the beauty of my own true nature. May my heart remain open. May I be healed."

This time, allow about six deep breaths—or as long as another ten minutes—in silence.

End the silence by praying the Lord's Prayer together. Then lead the group in whatever service you have selected from *The Book of Common Prayer.*

Focus: Journal Activities

Luke

Once again, unless you had a marathon session during which you read all of Luke aloud, you need to check in with any questions about what they read since the last session. After responding to any questions, simply go around the circle and ask each participant to read one quotation they recorded from Luke, even if half the people ahead of them recorded the same one. (It's always good to hear familiar stories.)

Sermon Notes

Then ask if anyone has comments, quotes or questions they want to share in connection with a recent sermon. If so, take the time to respond, encouraging others to participate.

Focus: Seeking and Serving Christ in Others

Storytelling

Remember that Jesus replaced all 613 laws from the old dispensation with only two: love God, and love your neighbor as yourself. Begin by reading the question that is the focus of this session:

> *Will you seek and serve Christ in all persons, loving your neighbor as yourself?*

By now they should know the appropriate response; if not, coach them:

> *I will, with God's help.*

(Remind them of the grace implied in their reply: they are not expected to do this alone, never alone, but always with God's help.)

Then go back to the stone-setting question about those who treated them well. Ask them to tell the stories surrounding those people. It is, after all, because we have experienced their caring for us that we know the kind of care we should be offering to others. Those people also helped us recognize our own belovedness: they offered a sampling of God's love for us.

After they have told their stories, point out that those people are all present among you at this session; their names have been built into the altar as participants set their stones. Suggest that they actually write a letter of appreciation to the person they named if that is a feasible option, or encourage them to add them to their prayers, thanking God for their caring witness.

Yarn Web

Then talk about the people who serve us daily in various capacities, from teachers to check-out clerks, workers at the power plant to farmers growing our food, those we interact with daily and those we never see. Human beings form a web of interconnectedness.

Read them John Donne's meditation. (The meditation is in their journals, but it deserves being heard aloud.) Explain that John Donne is honored by the Episcopal Church on March 31; he is part of our extended family. As Donne himself knew, we are all connected one to the other:

The church is catholic, universal, so are all her actions; all that she does pertains to all. When she baptizes a child, that action concerns me; for that child is thereby connected to that body which is my head too, and ingrafted into that body whereof I am a member. And when she buries a man, that action concerns me....No man is an island, entire of itself; every man is a piece of the continent, a part of the main.

Anyone's loss or anyone's gain affects us all. To demonstrate this interconnectedness, have everyone stand. (It might be safer to put the candle *under* the table for this exercise, but leave the stones in place.) Show them the ball of yarn and explain that you will toss it across the circle to one of the participants, speaking again the name of the person you credited with treating you well. Each person should hold the yarn briefly, think a brief prayer of gratitude, name their benefactor and toss the yarn to someone who hasn't yet held it. (Keep hold of the free end!)

Continue until all the participants are webbed together. The last participant should toss the ball of yarn back to you. As everyone stands there holding the web, tell them to think not only of those they named right now, but of all those who came to mind during meditation, of all the people with whom they are connected through love, through community, through life. Then offer prayer 54 from page 831 in the prayer book, "For those we Love":

Almighty God, we entrust all who are dear to us to your never-failing care and love, for this life and the life to come, knowing that you are doing for them better things than we can desire or pray for; through Jesus Christ our Lord. Amen.

By this time it's likely that people have forgotten from whom they got the yarn, so explain that as you perform this next prayer web, the person holding the yarn will need to tug it gently—hard tugs can pull the yarn out of someone's hand— and the one on the receiving end needs to indicate getting the tug. This time, as participants toss the yarn back to the one who tossed it to them, they should name someone they themselves have served as though Christ were present, someone they have treated well.

You begin. Tug the yarn to make sure who is on the other end. Name someone to whom you have been kind, helpful, compassionate. Then toss the ball of yarn. Whoever receives the ball needs to wind up the loose yarn before tossing it back to the previous person. Once everyone is done, and you have the complete ball of yarn back in your hands, hold it reverently, then place it on the table, reminding participants that all these people, too, are now present among you.

Intercessory Prayer

This would be a good time to look at intercessory prayer as a kind of service to ourselves and to our neighbors. If you have guest speakers, this would be an appropriate time to ask them to speak. If you have no speaker, or if you have time even after their presentation, turn to The Great Litany on page 148 in the prayer book; it has a sweeping inclusion of our fears as well as our desires as well as our prayers for others. If you feel pressed for time, use Form III of the Prayers of the People on page 387. (If you are covering this chapter in two sessions, this would be an appropriate time to close out this first session.)

Focus: Loving Our Neighbors as Ourselves

Caring for Self

The commandment Jesus gave us to love our neighbors as ourselves assumes that we do, indeed, care for and love ourselves. "This commandment implies that we should care for ourselves in body, mind, and spirit in order to show our love to others" (Tucker and Swatos 51). On the one hand, commercials such as those for the U. S. Army tell us to be "all we can be," while another voice of our culture tells us to *deny* ourselves for the sake of others.

Both, of course, are right. In order to be able to look after others, we need to be the person—the best person—God calls us to be. As Roberta Bondi says, "my life as a human being, made in the image of God, is holy because God loves it, and so in some mysterious way it is the site of God's beloved, holy presence" (46). And it is in this fullness of grace that we are then to go out and love others.

Take a few moments to stop here and ask participants to think of an adjective that describes their current state of being—an honest response to "How are you?" This can be anything from "hungry" to "stressed" to "really happy right now." Go quickly around the circle just getting responses without commentary.

Then ask group members to name one way in which they *care* for themselves. Again go quickly around the circle. Suggest that they take seriously the need to treat themselves as beloved children of God so that they might have the well-being and energy needed to serve God by serving others. It is, after all, through loving others that we actually show our love for God, just as Paul longed to care tenderly for the Thessalonians, like a nurse caring for her young.

Good Samaritan

The wording of the commandment in scripture is to love our "neighbor"; this raises the question of who our neighbors really are. When Lewis Sligh said "the person God puts in front of us is our neighbor," I wanted not to believe him. But I knew he was right. He means that the angry student who threatened to put my eye out with a pen is my neighbor. Hmm...

So is the tired bagger who squashed my grapes. So is my colleague whose E-mail calls for immediate response even though I have papers to grade and dinner to fix. Oh. It's not just the person in desperate need (which is how I've read the Parable of the Good Samaritan), but the person God puts in front of me, day by day by day.

If you have time and an outgoing group of participants, you might consider doing a dramatic reading of the Parable of the Good Samaritan, beginning at Luke 10:29. You will need one participant to take the part of the victim, several as robbers who attack him or her, a priest, a Levite, a Samaritan and an innkeeper. Or you can read the passage aloud, as you did the Parable of the Prodigal Son. Read it once or twice slowly, giving participants time to record words, phrases or images that strike them as you read.

To reinforce the message about honoring Christ in those God puts in front of us, read to your participants these excerpts from "Visitation," a short story by the Rev. Bob Jewett:

> Sure 'n it's a grand old buildin' indeed," Mrs. Marshall thought to herself, as she stood in the marbled entrance hall... She peered out the door's window at the grand stairway. "Empty! Not a soul in sight yet, praise be! There's still time t' get ready..."
>
> Nervously she turned back to recheck the street and was stunned by bumping directly into a figure she hadn't heard come into the foyer behind her.
>
> "Mother o' God! Who'er you now!?" she demanded. Taking a half-step back, she was chagrined to see a tawdry, disheveled street woman standing expressionless before her, smack in the middle of the grand hallway...
>
> "Oh no, Missus. Not today y' don't," sighed Mrs. Marshall... "Y'see: the Queen's t' come today. T' see our program and how we serve the folks as come here f'r their needs, if y' know what I mean." She tried to shuffle the bag-lady toward the entrance.
>
> But the woman was immovable.
>
> Mrs. M pushed harder.
>
> The woman quirked a half-smile of embarrassed intransigence. She was not to be turned away. "But, Mum. If you please, just let me sit quiet in a corner there. I shan't bother no one. No one at all." She began to slump down, as though to collapse right there on the marble floor.
>
> "No. It just cannot be. Not today," Mrs. M continued. "I'm ever so sorry." But her tone suggested a lorry driver's frustrated rage at sheep blocking his roadway, rather than the compromised, over-committed program directress she was.
>
> "But Mum, m' feet! They'll carry me no furtha' this day. It's 'ere, 'tis. Or 'ospital, f'r sure. There's nary 'nother mile in them boots, indeed! 'Ere or 'ospital. That's it."
>
> "Well. Well, all right," surrendered Mrs. M, glancing over her shoulder for another peek at the street outside. She turned the old woman around and shuffled her quickly

to a table at the very back of the Hall. "Sit here. One o' mi girls will bring y' a cup-a-tea. Now," she said officiously shaking her finger at the woman, "nary bother, mind y'!" Abruptly she turned, sliding quickly away to her tasks.

At last a movement down the street caught her eye, and she slid quickly to the center doorway. "Finally! Finally!" and she straightened imperceptibly the skirt of her midnight-blue flannel suit. "Here they come indeed!" ...Chauffeurs from each limousine leapt from behind the wheel and snappily circled to the curbside...

Where is She?" Mrs. M muttered under her breath, her heart pounding.

[A] professional man checked his pocket-watch, shook his head, and began to step briskly up the stairway toward Mrs. Marshall. She thought she remembered now that this one was the Queen's own physician, who customarily attended her at public functions. At the head of the stairway Mrs. Marshall extended her hand professionally to welcome the doctor and query the Queen's whereabouts...

But suddenly a commotion erupted from the Great Hall... the sound of shattering china and a woman's scream pierced the air...

They pushed through the shifting crowd, and Mrs. M kept mumbling—more to herself than to anyone around her, "And where is She anyway? Haven't I done ev'rything I could t'make all ready? Haven't I planned and cooked and cleaned and polished and set up this entire place just f'r Her. And where is She anyway? When will She arrive?..."

They broke through the circle surrounding the table at the rear of the hall... The gaunt physician knelt beside the old bag-lady sprawled unrecognizably on the floor. As he felt for her pulse, his eyes, deeply concerned, looked up to arrest Mrs. Marshall in her place.

"It is the Queen!" he breathed....

Remember that Jesus says whatever we do for the least and the lowest, we do for him; what we deny another, we deny him. We serve others—tattered or regal—because Christ dwells in them. Sligh tells of Mother Teresa speaking to her sisters at the end of the day saying, "Jesus had running sores today. Jesus couldn't keep any gruel down today." She not only *served* Christ in others, but named his presence there. "Jesus was angry today," she said, and I think of my angry, hurting student.

Jesus is my neighbor. My neighbor is whoever God sets before me each day. This is hard. Tell the participants that you are going to ask them a hard question—but it's one that their journals have been asking them, so they should be prepared: "Where was Jesus today?" (Another way of phrasing it is "Who did God give me as my neighbor today?") Be honest in your own response, and then elicit theirs.

Lewis Sligh names the great heresy of our times as apathy. If one becomes un-apathetic, however, the vast troubles of the world can be overwhelming, numbing, sending one immediately back into apathy. We are, however, incarnated, placed in a certain venue, Sligh reminds us, and *that* is where we are called to do our work. That's why Sligh is so insistent that our neighbors are those God puts before us day by day. Christians "are those who come forth to be disciples...to be yoked, to serve those whom he serves" (Willimon 21).

Footwashing

The dominant symbolic gesture of Jesus' servant ministry is his washing of the disciples' feet. The Maundy Thursday service in *The Book of Common Prayer*, *The Book of Occasional Services* and the *Journey to Adulthood* program all include footwashing as a symbolic ritual of servanthood. (Also, since this whole program is designed to help participants prepare to renew baptismal vows, any chance to splash about in water is a good thing.)

Marianne Micks compares Jesus' footwashing to baptism when He tells Peter, "Unless I wash you, you have no share with me" and Peter exclaims, "Lord, not my feet only but also my hands and my head!" (This passage, by the way, offers an alternative if footwashing seems an impossible endeavor: wash one another's hands using the pitcher of water, the bowl and soft towels. This is what we do on Maundy Thursday at St. Paul's in Brunswick, often a bleak, winter-feeling night in Maine when baring one's booted feet would be a frigid and time-consuming chore.)

In the Maundy Thursday rite in the *Book of Occasional Services*, those preparing to renew baptismal vows are the first to get their feet washed, after which the celebrant gives them the basins and towels, speaks these words to them: "May Christ strengthen you in the service which he lays upon you," and sends them off to wash the feet of the other members of the congregation (145).

Do the foot (or hand) washing. Don't skip this activity. If you are musical (or the participants are) ask them to quietly sing a repetitive anthem or hymn during the process, or play a tape of sacred music. This will promote a meditative atmosphere and avoid some of the possible embarrassment surrounding the footwashing. Appropriate hymns from *The Hymnal 1982* include:

"God is love" (#576, 577)
"Where true charity and love dwell" (#606)
"Seek ye first the kingdom of God" (#711)

Move from the footwashing into your customary closing activities.

Focus: The Next Session

Prayer Cards

Once again, ask participants to get out their prayer card with a participant's name, to turn it over and write, "You have been in my prayers," then to sign their names and pass the card to the person on their right. (If some end up with their own names, tell them to be especially conscious of praying for themselves this time; next time they will pass the card on. Praying either for oneself or for another group member is equally appropriate after this particular session.)

Closing

Close this session as you have the others with the prayer "For those about to be Baptized or to renew their Baptismal Covenant" on page 819 of the prayer book:

> O God, you prepared your disciples for the coming of your Spirit through the teaching of your Son Jesus Christ: Make the hearts and minds of your servants ready to receive the blessing of the Holy Spirit, that they may be filled with his presence; through Jesus Christ our Lord. Amen.

Then stand and sing your chosen hymn or recite the chosen canticle.

Have participants retrieve their chosen stones and step back into the circle.

Conclude with the exchange of the peace:

> Leader: The peace of the Lord be always with you.
> Participants: And also with you.

Blow out the candle.

After the Session

Looking Back, Looking Forward

Once all the participants have left, allow yourself a brief moment of reflection.

Where did you particularly feel God's grace among you during this session?

....

....

....

....

....

....

What do you wish had happened that didn't—or what did happen that you wish hadn't?

....

....

....

....

....

Offer it all to God, both the gracious and the grueling.

Be open to feel God's gratitude for your time and for your caring.

Go in peace, knowing that you have served God well.

Into the World in Witness

PLAN THE SESSION

Celebrant: **"Will you strive for justice and peace among all people, and respect the dignity of every human being?"**

People: *"I will, with God's help."*

To Bring

- a candle and matches
- the communal psalm
- index cards
- pens and pencils
- extra Bibles
- prayer books (encourage participants to bring their own)
- leftover stones
- a watch if needed
- any memorabilia you might have (t-shirts, bookmarks— whatever is affordable and accessible)

Optional:
- "bread for the journey": baked goods to share as a final "meal" together (You may wish to enlist parish help for this.)

Matters of Time

Single session: This chapter has fewer specific activities. Since this is the last session of the program, more time is provided to reach closure with each of the established rituals.

Two sessions: If you divide this into two sessions, do the ritual and activity component the first session and a field trip the second. See the "longer/retreat session" section for suggestions.

Longer/retreat session: What would, of course, be most appropriate for this session on peace and justice—which is also the last official session—would be to leave the place of your usual gathering after the closing ritual and literally go into the world as witnesses, i.e., go to a local place that promotes the respect and dignity of every person. If participants have all been serving one particular local agency, go there as a group.

Other options include anything from Hospice, with its gentle respect for the dying, to a soup kitchen or food pantry, a shelter for the homeless, Meals on Wheels, a setting where literacy is encouraged or whatever agency, organization or individual involved in service that you can find. Bishop Chilton Knudsen says that when confirmands say "Yes, I'll respect others," those "others" need to be more than their own peer group. It's easy to respect people like ourselves. Instead, Knudsen says we should "go to people whose freedom and dignity aren't so evident," and respect them, too. And not just to serve them, but to encounter and respect their dignity as human beings.

Bishop Knudsen urges confirmands to have an afternoon and evening retreat—perhaps even an overnight vigil—the day before confirmation. This retreat would be for participants, leaders, sponsors, mentors and even the bishop. The Epilogue encourages you to have gatherings of the group a month or so *after* they actually renew their Baptismal Covenant, and again a full year later. If this isn't feasible, suggest that participants write a letter to you as a way of ongoing witness. These follow-up activities will give participants a chance to reflect on the whole experience. It also reminds them that confirmation is not graduation but a promise of renewed commitment.

The Session(s) at a Glance

Gather

- light the candle
- set the stones
- read together the communal psalm
- maintain short silence
- share the appropriate service from *The Book of Common Prayer*

Activities

- focus on journal activities
  — reflections on Luke
  — reflections on sermon notes

- focus on respecting dignity
  - — stories of peace and justice
  - — ministry to the stranger
  - — political concerns
- focus on closure
  - — prayer cards
  - — final activities

Closing

- sing chosen hymn or recite chosen canticle
- retrieve stones
- remind group members to finish their journals between sessions
- exchange peace
- blow out candle
- go into the world in witness

Leader's Reflection

This chapter deals with striving for justice and peace, with respecting human dignity. This is when I would call up a member of the outreach committee of my parish and ask their advice. If your parish has a social action or peace and justice group, solicit their input. This session's baptismal promise is a promise that needs to be kept through action—"striving"—rather than through discussion. Prayer in this case needs to be accompanied by involvement.

Bishop Knudsen hopes that a confirmation program would not only include group spiritual direction and discussion, but would also have a service component through which confirmands undertake "ministry to the stranger." Ideally, participants in this program have been doing some sort of outside service through a local organization. Somehow those participating in this program need to see that they can make a difference through active striving.

Look back over your own life and ponder the various times and ways in which you have "ministered to the stranger." List them.

....
....
....
....
....
....
....
....

Now think about the issue of respecting every person's dignity. Think back to early childhood taunts, to casual adolescent cruelties, to current gossip, to remarks said or merely thought. What are some of your most egregious failures to respect someone's basic human dignity?

....
....
....
....
....

Who were those people you disrespected? Were they friends, family, colleagues, strangers? What led you to think or act as you did?

....
....
....
....
....

Do you still think and act that way? If not (or not as much), what changed you?

....
....
....
....
....

Be ready to help your participants deal with these hard questions. Commend effort to change. Be gentle with them as with yourself while still encouraging the striving.

Be Tender to Yourself

As you near the end of your leadership of this particular group, allow yourself to feel God's gratitude for the work you have done. Remember that you are a child of God, infinitely loved and precious. No matter how this final session goes, God is still and always at work among you, and all will be well.

What are your biggest fears or biggest hopes for this final session? Write them below, and offer them to God.

....

....

....

....

....

Before the Session

Arrange the field trip—or the invitation for a "stranger" to come among you. My high school has invited persons with AIDS to speak to students. In mostly-white Maine, an African-American teenager spoke to one of my American literature classes about her experiences, not only in the south, but in their own town. The gay/straight student alliance held an afternoon of readings and music at my school.

Confronting in person those whose dignity is sometimes called into question gives a human face to the label, and encourages us to accord them respect. Not to do so breaks our baptismal vow. If arranging for everyone to go together on a "field trip" in search of justice and peace isn't feasible, bring the "stranger" to them.

Meanwhile, set up the space as usual. If you aren't going to have retreat time the day or evening before the actual service, it might be good to break bread together this last session, to be reminded of one another's companionship ("with-bread-ness") on this journey you've shared. This might be something parishioners could provide, some kind of baked goods for this farewell: "bread for the journey."

If you have a visitor coming in, arrange for that person to speak to the group right after setting the stones; be sure you have a stone for the visitor to "build into the altar." This allows the group to reach closure together afterwards. If you are going out into the community, that could be done either before or after the actual session. The symbolic nature of finishing the session and then going into the world is very appealing, but the timing may not allow for this possibility. Do what will work best for your group.

THE SESSION

Gather

Once everyone has arrived, gather in a circle around the table. Tell the participants that once you have lit the candle, they should step forward, set their stone, and as they say their names, they should follow up by answering the question, "Where did you strive for justice and peace this week?" Give them examples: "Susan Omori. I strove for justice and peace when I took my turn at the soup kitchen." "Lawrence Little Thunder. I gave money to the Presiding Bishop's Fund for disaster relief." "Maria Palma. I sat with a new student during lunch."

If you have a visitor, be sure to offer a stone. Light the candle. Name yourself. Name one way you strove for justice and peace this week. Then let the others follow.

Once everyone has helped "build the altar" this week, sit down. If you have a visitor, invite that person to share his or her story with the group. Allow time for questions. Model respectful attention. Invite the visitor to stay through the psalm, the silence and the service. If he or she chooses not to, offer deep gratitude for the courage and time to come among you as a "stranger," and bid farewell.

Ask participants to get out their copy of the communal psalm. Ask the group members to find a comfortable sitting position and breathe deeply. Lead them in a final recitation, in whatever creative manner you choose.

> Leader: The Lord be with you.
> Participants: And also with you.
> Leader: Let us pray.

Pray the psalm. Then enter into silence.

End the silence by praying the Lord's Prayer together. Then lead the group in whatever service you have selected ahead of time from *The Book of Common Prayer*. After the service, if the visitor has stayed, this would be an appropriate time to bid him or her a grateful farewell before moving on.

Focus: Journal Activities

Luke

By now, all the participants should have finished Luke. Ask for final comments, questions and quotations. You might at this time share some of your own favorite passages from Luke.

Sermon Notes

Then ask if anyone has comments, quotations or questions they want to share in connection with a recent sermon. If so, take the time to respond, encouraging others to join in. Suggest that for the rest of their lives they listen to sermons with the same attentiveness, always open to hearing the Word of God spoken anew.

Focus: Respecting Dignity

Stories of Peace and Justice

In his volume of the Church's New Teaching Series, Johnston says that Mark's gospel is "unequivocal" that "the discipleship community welcomes the stranger." Membership in the Christian community, he says, "has consequences...the terms are non-negotiable...individual autonomy is not a Christian virtue" (82). Going back to the first session: there's no such thing as a solitary Christian. Not only is that a comforting statement, it is also one that demands responsibility.

The Rev. Lewis Sligh speaks of having a revelation of Jesus while standing in line waiting among relatively affluent Washingtonians to see the two-person comedy *A Tuna Christmas*. A homeless man approached the line and began specifically asking for money. Conversation stopped. When people denied him money, they wouldn't even look at him. "It's almost like they have a disease we don't want to catch. The homeless are the lepers of our time," Sligh says.

Sligh admits that some panhandlers use the money for drugs or alcohol, but he remembers that C.S. Lewis *always* gave some money because he was never sure which ones were real. (Remember Bob Jewett's story of the Queen). "What if I deny Jesus?" Sligh doesn't necessarily advocate giving to every request, but he does insist on our need to give charitable donations of time, money and resources to local agencies. "We have *huge* global problems that we can't solve all at once, but we *can* make a difference if we live with intention at the immediate level."

Ellen Charry says that Christians "are surrounded by God's grace...they have become instruments of divine grace, ambassadors for Christ, messengers of reconciliation" (*By* 58). Sligh tells the story of a high school boy in the Tampa Bay area who realized that at the end of the school day they were throwing away food. He began collecting it and taking it to the local soup kitchen.

Eventually the boy involved his friends, and then he got the whole school district involved. Local restaurants began to contribute, too. One tenth grader was able to change the way an entire community worked. "[T]he living presence of God here and now, in this world, in *exactly* this world, as men know it and touch it and smell it and live and work in it" is where William Stringfellow told Christians to witness. That compassionate young man did.

Take time now to ask participants to tell the stories that go with their stones: how they have striven for peace and justice this week.

After they have finished, ask them to turn to prayer 62 on page 833 in the prayer book: it is the St. Francis prayer of self-dedication. Pray it together in unison. Then pause a moment in silence.

Political Concerns

Mention that besides our work at the immediate level, we can even make our voices heard on global issues through political activity. Suggest that participants get in the habit of writing to senators and members of Congress about issues dealing with human dignity and justice, sending copies of their letters to the local paper.

The Christians who signed the Theological Declaration of Barmen early in World War II publicly separated themselves from Hitler's "German Church," utterly rejecting the human arrogance that was perverting the church to serve the Third Reich. They wrote: "we may not keep silent...in a time of common need and temptation...even risking lives..." We, too, may not keep silent when we recognize evil, when we see people's respect and dignity denied.

When the Rt. Rev. George Cadigan was Bishop of Missouri during the 1960s and early 70s, he sometimes got in trouble with his own parishes for speaking out on anti-semitism, racism and the war in Vietnam. After sending pastoral letters on these issues, he would often get phone calls at 2 a.m., trash thrown on his lawn, but he persevered. He never got angry at those in opposition, never challenged them. Like the sun in the story of the North Wind and the Sun, he loved them back.

For as long as twenty years afterwards, he continued to receive letters from people saying, "You were right," people who had left the church in anger and come back. Be willing to speak out, he says. Follow your conscience.

What Bishop Cadigan sees as the social justice issue of current times is the treatment of gays and lesbians. Lewis Sligh tells of a church in Georgia, for example, that allows people to have pets in the pictorial directory, but not same-sex partners. "They bless animals on St. Francis Day, but won't bless gay couples." In public school teaching I hear more derogatory homophobic language than other kinds of verbal abuse. Since a recent harassment policy is in place there is less of it, but a damaging undercurrent remains which would deny the basic human dignity of those under attack.

Ask your participants what ethnic, social or other groups suffer the most disrespect; then brainstorm ways to counteract such verbal abuse. As Bishop Cadigan says, "We need to know we are loved by Almighty God." We need to restore the dignity of those denied it, to offer respect even for the stranger and outsider, so that through us they might feel the love of Christ.

Ministry to the Stranger

If your participants have been engaged in "ministry to the stranger" throughout their preparation, take time now to discuss their experiences. If they haven't, use this time to prepare them for where you will be going or to review what your visitor said earlier.

Focus: Closure

Prayer Cards

One last time, ask participants to get out their prayer card with a participant's name, to turn it over and write, "You have been in my prayers" then to sign their names and pass the card to its owner. Ask them to continue to pray for you and for one another as they await the bishop's visit.

Final Activities

Remind them to complete their Spiritual Journey in their journals before they renew their Baptismal Covenant.

If there is to be a retreat, a shared meal or an all-night vigil prior to the service, give them the details; a printed invitation would be a nice touch.

If you plan a "reunion" in another month or so, set that up now as well. Consider issuing a formal invitation now with a follow-up phone call or mailing closer to the date itself.

If the parish has provided you with food to share at this final meeting, allow time to enjoy it before closing. The group should be comfortable enough by now not to need directed conversation. If you have memorabilia (besides the stones) for the participants, this would be a good time to distribute such items.

Closing

Close this session as you have the others with the prayer "For those about to be Baptized or to renew their Baptismal Covenant" on page 819 of the prayer book:

> *O God, you prepared your disciples for the coming of your Spirit through the teaching of your Son Jesus Christ: Make the hearts and minds of your servants ready to receive the blessing of the Holy Spirit, that they may be filled with his presence; through Jesus Christ our Lord. Amen.*

Then have participants turn to the "Prayers for the Candidates" on page 305 in the prayer book. Omit the Celebrant's words and pray the Leader's words, inviting the participants to respond as the People.

Then sing your chosen hymn or recite the chosen canticle.

Have participants retrieve their chosen stones and step back into the circle.

Conclude with the exchange of the peace:

> *Leader:* The peace of the Lord be always with you.
> *Participants:* And also with you.

Blow out the candle.

Whether you are now leaving with the participants to go out into the community and "minister to the stranger," or whether you have had a visitor and are saying good-bye to the participants, stand by the door and send them out joyfully with the words, "Into the world in witness!"

After the Session

Looking Back, Looking Forward

Once you finally have time, allow yourself an extended period of reflection.

Where did you particularly feel God's grace among you during this final session?

....

....

....

....

....

If you lead this program in the future, what do you want to be sure to repeat that worked well?

....

....

....

....

....

What would you have done differently? If you lead this program again, what will you change?

....

....

....

....

Be open to feel God's gratitude for your time and for your caring.

Go in peace, knowing that you have served God well.

Epilogue

Having prepared your participants, now what? What should be done to prepare for the service itself?

Bishop Knudsen speaks of a "high doctrine of confirmation" that would honor confirmation with as spectacular a liturgy as ordination, since both sacraments are ones that commission us for ministry. (Many liturgical scholars, however, would caution against according *either* of these liturgies more attention than the sacrament of baptism itself. It is baptism that fully invites us into full ministry.) In confirmation, the confirmands "stand on their own two feet" and choose to say "yes" to God's call to membership and ministry.

In a perfect world, Knudsen says, all confirmations would be regional. The combined choirs of the various churches involved would rehearse together, and plans for the after-party would engage the energy and imagination of all the involved parishes. Regional confirmations are the norm in many dioceses already.

The Rev. Vicki Sirota, for example, took her inner city confirmands to a middle class African-American church for a regional confirmation. At first her group felt out of place, but when the liturgy began "they knew it; they realized they were at home." Because confirmation connects the confirmands to the wider Church through the laying on of hands, the movement to regional confirmations (which in their very numbers and diversity would incarnate the wider Church) seems appropriate. "To be an Episcopalian," says Bishop Knudsen, "is to be a person of infinite relatedness."

And after the service? "Don't let confirmation become graduation!" Jane Hartwell pleads. "The call of God takes time," says Sam Portaro, "and to answer takes even more time" (37). "Faith is a history new every morning," writes Karl Barth (*Evangelical Theology*, 103). Trinity's Confirmation Task Force comments that "Our development as Christians is a journey, an ongoing process that is the work of a lifetime." What all these folks are saying is that confirmation is only a beginning, that answering "yes" to God takes a lifetime, not a single Sunday afternoon.

Sam Portaro goes on to say that "Because of his profound responsibility, Jesus is tempted as soon as he has been baptized" (43). Your participants have built up a readiness for the sacrament of confirmation. What they still need is strength to continue their "yes" in the months and years after the ceremony is over. Temptation will happen. "Jesus learns that the willing acceptance of responsibility for one's life is not the end of it; it is only the beginning, as the wilderness experience proves" (Portaro 43).

This is why I strongly urge you to have plans for a follow-up gathering in a month or so firmly in place before you send your participants out into the world at the end of the last session. This follow-up gathering should be a simple repeat of your standard opening, complete with lighting a candle, setting the stones, praying the communal psalm, silence and a service.

After that, share a meal—or just coffee and pastries— accompanied by questions such as "How's it going?" or "What's it been like since...?" Tell them about Jesus' temptations coming immediately after his baptism. Ask if they have faced unusual temptations, endured any "wilderness experiences." Remind them of Paul's reassuring words that they copied down at the very first session: read them aloud. Close the gathering with your familiar hymn or canticle and the exchange of the peace.

These participants have become yours; as the fox reminded the Little Prince: you are responsible one for the other forever. If it feels appropriate, establish another follow-up around the anniversary of their confirmation (reception or reaffirmation). If that seems an impossibility, at the month-later gathering tell them that you will be sending them a letter in a year—and then make sure you do it!

In such a letter, you can greet them graciously, ask for an update on their spiritual well-being and their church and community involvement, commend their group members and yourself to their prayers, and offer a prayer for them. Include a stamped, self-addressed envelope (what would really be nice would be to enclose not only an envelope but a blank card for them to write on—even if just an index card in memory of this program's exercises).

At whatever serves as the final gathering of this group, be it the last session or a follow-up meeting, give each participant a candle with a handwritten note that says: "You are Christ's witnesses to the ends of the earth. You are the light of the world."

Give yourself a candle, too. You have been God's witness. You have lit up God's world with your time and energy and caring for this group.

May the peace of the Lord be always with you. Amen.

BIBLIOGRAPHY

Barth, Karl. *Church Dogmatics: A Selection*, Louisville: Westminster John Knox Press, 1994.

Barth, Karl. *Evangelical Theology: An Introduction*. Trans. Grover Foley. Grand Rapids: William B. Eerdmans Publishing Company, 1988.

Barth, Karl. *Final Testimonies*. Trans. Geoffrey W. Bromiley. Grand Rapids: William B. Eerdmans Publishing Company, 1997..

Barth, Karl. *The Preaching of the Gospel*. Trans. B. E. Hooke. Philadelphia: The Westminster Press, 1963.

Bondi, Roberta. *A Place to Pray*. Nashville: Abingdon Press, 1998.

The Book of Occasional Services. New York: Church Publishing Inc., 1995.

Brown, Raymond E. *A Risen Christ in Eastertime*. Collegeville MN: The Liturgical Press, 1991.

The Catechumenal Process: Adult Initiation and Formation for Christian Life and Ministry. New York: The Church Hymnal Corp., 1990.

Charry, Ellen. *By the Renewing of Your Minds*. New York: Oxford University Press, 1997.

Charry, Ellen and Dana Charry. "Send a Christian to Camp." *The Christian Century*, vol.116:20. 14-21 July, 1999: 708-710.

Cunningham, Mary Kathleen. *What Is Theological Exegesis?* Valley Forge: Trinity Press International, 1995.

Deck, Sylvia Cirone. *Ministry of Hospitality*. Kansas City: Sheed & Ward, 1996.

Easley, Julia. "Evangelism with Young Adults." *Resource Book for Ministries with Youth and Young Adults in the Episcopal Church*. Ed. Sheryl Kujawa and Lois Sibley. New York: Episcopal Church Center, 1995.

Farrer, Austin. *Lord I Believe*. Cambridge: Cowley Publications, 1989.

Ferlo, Roger. *Opening the Bible: The Church's New Teaching Series Vol. 2*. Cambridge: Cowley Publications, 1997.

Griffiss, James E. *The Anglican Vision: The Church's New Teaching Series Vol 1*. Cambridge: Cowley Publications, 1997.

Harrington, Daniel J., SJ. "New Testament Perspectives on the Ministry of the Word." *Chicago Studies* vol. 13:1 Spring 1974: 65-76.

Hartwell, Herbert. *The Theology of Karl Barth*. Philadelphia: The Westminster Press, 1964.

Johnston, Michael. *Engaging the Word: The Church's New Teaching Series Vol. 3*. Cambridge: Cowley Publications, 1998.

Lee, Jeffrey. *Opening the Prayer Book: The Church's New Teaching Series Vol. 7*. Cambridge: Cowley Publications, 1999.

Lowry, Charles W. *The Trinity and Christian Devotion*. New York: Harper & Brothers, 1946.

Micks, Marianne. *Deep Waters: An Introduction to Baptism*. Cambridge: Cowley Publications, 1996.

Mitchell, Leonel L. *Praying Shapes Believing: a Theological Commentary on the Book of Common Prayer*. Minneapolis: Winston Press, 1985.

Mitchell, Leonel L. "What Shall We Do about Confirmation?" *A Prayer Book for the 21st Century: Liturgical Studies 3*. New York: The Church Hymnal Corp., 1996.

A New Zealand Prayer Book. He Karakia Mihinare o Aotearoa. San Francisco: HarperSan Francisco, 1997.

Plater, Ormonde. *Intercession*. Cambridge: Cowley Publications, 1995.

Portaro, Sam. *Crossing the Jordan*. Cambridge: Cowley Publications, 1999.

A Prayer Book for Australia. Alexandria NSW: Braughton Books, 1996.

Romero, Oscar. *The Violence of Love*. Compiled and trans. James R. Brockman, SJ. Farmington PA: The Plough Publishing House, 1998.

Runia, Klaus. *Karl Barth's Doctrine of Holy Scripture*. Grand Rapids: William B. Eerdmans Publishing Company, 1962.

Sayers, Dorothy L. *Creed or Chaos?* Manchester NH: Sophia Institute Press, 1995.

Shannon, William H. *Seeking the Face of God*. New York: Crossroad, 1990.

Standing Liturgical Commission. *Holy Baptism together with A Form of Confirmation or the Laying-on- of Hands by the Bishop with the Affirmation of Baptismal Vows, as authorized by the General Convention of 1973. Prayer Book Studies 26*. New York: The Church Hymnal Corp., 1973.

Taylor, Barbara Brown. *The Preaching Life*. Cambridge: Cowley Publications, 1993.

Tucker, Beverly D. and William H. Swatos, Jr. *Questions on the Way: A Catechism Based on the Book of Common Prayer*. Cincinnati: Forward Movement Publications, 1995.

Whitehead, Evelyn Eaton and James D. Whitehead. *Community of Faith*. Minneapolis: The Winston Seabury Press, 1982.

Willimon, William H. *What's Right with the Church?* San Francisco: Harper & Row, 1985.

Wright, N. T. *The Lord and His Prayer*. Cincinnati: Forward Movement Publications, 1996.